]

From t.

to the Living Room

"Our family certainly benefits from the Sandler communucation principles. This book is an inspiration, one that will help guide others to communicate more effectively with family and friends."

—Blain Tiffany
Metals Industry Executive

FROM THE
BOARD ROOM
TO THE
LIVING ROOM

FROM THE
BOARD ROOM
TO THE
LIVING ROOM

DAVID A. HIATT

Paperback: 978-0-692-07779-5

E-book: 978-0-692-07780-1

This book is dedicated to my loving wife Debi.
Without her, I would not have walked the path in life
leading me to this project. With the blessings of her support,
her patience, and her willingness to engage in insightful
conversations, I have been able to achieve a lifelong goal
and write this book. Thank you, my love.

CONTENTS

Acknowledgments . . . . *xiii*

Foreword . . . . *xv*

Introduction. . . . . *xvii*

CHAPTER 1: The Need. 1

    Changing the Outcome 1

    All Works in Progress 8

CHAPTER 2: The Skills 9

    Relating to People 9

    Communication Pie 10

    VAK 15

    Behavioral Styles. 18

    Transactional Analysis 28

    Connect to the Other Person. 37

    OK/Not-OK Theory 39

    More Positive Outcomes 42

CHAPTER 3: The Art of Mutual Agreements 45

    Starting the Conversation 45

    The Five Key Components: PLATE 54

    Mutual Agreement. 56

CHAPTER 4: Questions 57

The Pitfalls of Asking Questions 57

Questioning Strategies and Techniques 64

The Importance of Questions 84

CHAPTER 5: Listen and Talk 85

Listening: The Art of Paying Attention 85

Active Listening. 88

Talking: The Art of Self-Awareness 98

Words Are Labels 100

Pay Attention 102

CHAPTER 6: The Attitude 103

Attitude Is Mental. 103

Born a "10" 104

Childhood Conditioning 108

Beliefs 110

Comfort Zones 112

You Get What You Expect. 113

CHAPTER 7: Emotional Involvement 115

The Emotional Mind. 115

Keep Your Belly-Button Covered 117

It's Your Choice 120

Choose the Right Brain. 122

CHAPTER 8: The Outcomes. 123

Managing Outcomes 123

Outcomes Are a Choice 125

Take Control of the Outcomes. 127

CHAPTER 9: Growing Together. 129

Building Relationships 129

Interpersonal Goals 133

Develop Relationships 138

CHAPTER 10: Keep Talking 139

ADULT 141

Keep Talking!. 145

APPENDIX: The Art of De-escalation 147

ACKNOWLEDGMENTS

My gratitude goes out, first and foremost, to all the clients I've worked with over the years who shared good questions and good ideas, who told me how Sandler changed their lives for the better, and who challenged me to help them share this information with family members, friends, and loved ones. There are far too many of you to name here, but please accept my sincere thanks. I wrote this book because of you—and for you.

I'm also deeply grateful to everyone who helped in production and took care of all the details that I wouldn't have been able to keep track of, notably: Yusuf Toropov, Rachel Miller, Laura Matthews, Lori Ames, Jerry Dorris, Désirée Pilachowski, Deb Jordan, and Jennifer Willard.

For their early support and feedback, I want to thank

Diane Henriques, Julia Dalton, Bill Art, Lindsay Hiatt, and Ed Staub.

Special thanks are due to my sons, Michael and Brian, who have helped me grasp the importance of understanding the other person's perspective before making judgments.

For their ongoing support throughout the project, I am grateful to Margaret Stevens Jacks, Chip Doyle, Ken Channell, Debi Hiatt, and especially David Mattson for having faith in me throughout our friendship, which now spans more than two decades.

FOREWORD

At Sandler Training, one of the reactions we often get from our clients sounds something like this: "What you taught me about interacting with prospects and customers made a major positive impact on my sales career—and that's what I was hoping for. What I didn't expect, though, was that the Sandler® techniques and principles would improve my relationships with friends and family in such a dramatic way. Thank you."

Over the years, we've gotten that kind of feedback from literally thousands of people. Many of them have suggested that we publish a book summarizing our founder David Sandler's insights on effective communication and target the book not toward salespeople, but toward a general non-business audience. When it came time to choose the right author for such a book, Dave Hiatt was the obvious choice because of his deep familiarity with the material and his ability to offer a wealth of practical insights and examples beyond the world of business.

This book is the culmination of a long-term effort to carry the career-changing, life-changing Sandler concepts beyond our traditional audience. Dave has done a great job of fulfilling that assignment, and I know David Sandler would be proud of the result.

David Mattson
President/CEO, Sandler Training

INTRODUCTION

Long ago when my wife asked me where I would like to go for dinner, it was the beginning of my realizing much of our day-to-day communication is persuasion.

I made the mistake of suggesting a place in which she was not interested. I then suggested another place for dinner, which was also discounted. Finally, after my third strike, I realized she had a place in mind and was hoping I was going to suggest that place.

If I had been able to read her mind and suggest the right place, I would have believed that I had a say in where we were going for dinner. It could even have felt like my idea! I have since learned. She generally has a place in mind, is persuading me to go out for dinner, and wants to go to the place of her choice. Now I know. Since I love her and we've developed lots of communication patterns over the years, I am usually OK with all the above. For some people, though, this would be a problem. Communication can either bring us together or rip us apart.

You would think this would have been clear to me since I have spent my adult life studying and helping people, especially salespeople, to communicate more efficiently and effectively. Most of the help I've offered has been in the business world. It makes sense to up your communication game for more positive outcomes regarding commerce. But now and then a client would share with me how the lessons learned in my sessions had improved their personal life as well. Many of the hundreds of my fellow trainers throughout the world report similar feedback.

I knew I had to write this book when a client said to me, "I wish my wife and kids could learn this communication stuff. She could improve her work relationship and my kids would be more equipped to communicate with adults as they try to get into college or even get a job." The comment from another client pushed me over the top to begin writing when she said, "Thank you, Dave. You saved my marriage!" I thought, *Wow! I am not even a marriage counselor. This is some powerful stuff.*

So, this book is for all of you who want to improve your relationships with family, friends, coworkers, and customers—and are willing to take the responsibility to make it happen.

In this book I have tried to capture the communication concepts, strategies, and tactics that help in the world of business but also allow for conversations at home and in the workplace to flow smoothly. I have learned that mastering communication skills is a lifelong process, and at any point in time there is room for improvement. Most of my communication knowledge comes from bachelor's and master's degrees in communications with a minor in psychology and from over 23 years of coaching salespeople in the Sandler Selling System® methodology. My goal in this book is to share decades of learning and teaching effective and efficient communication skills with you. I want to help you communicate better.

My hope is you can use these concepts, strategies, and tactics to improve your personal communication skills with your family, friends, coworkers, and customers to achieve more positive outcomes.

CHAPTER 1

The Need

Changing the Outcome

There are many situations with family, friends, coworkers, bosses, or neighbors that require you to be the bigger person. You cannot always get others to agree with you. Sometimes they are obstinate and become a roadblock. Other times you are the roadblock. As you read this chapter, think of the times when you needed to communicate more effectively with the other person. Ask yourself this: "Could I have changed the outcome to be more positive?" When thinking about specific instances, perhaps the thought came, "I shouldn't have said anything." Let's explore why people need the tools to make the right communication choices.

Alert!

Silence might be the right choice.

Significant Other

Looking back on failed relationships (and most people have one or two), you can usually recall a specific conversation, or lack of conversation, as the pivotal moment in the relationship's end. The self-talk usually ends with, "If I am not listened to or taken seriously there is no future in this relationship." If you could read the other person's mind, you would probably discover their self-talk told them the same.

Of course, people also have relationships that work out and endure. Even in those relationships, the bumpy roads are navigated successfully when each one makes the effort to truly listen and understand each other. It is the extra effort made to communicate with each other that usually saves the relationship.

I can remember one of my close friends telling me about a time when he and his wife were going through a rough patch—a rough patch far enough along to talk with lawyers. As I recall his story, his wife was the one who said, "Do you truly want to do this?" His response was a definite, "No!" They agreed to talk it out and go through each of the issues, one by one, so they could figure out if they would be able to resolve them or not. I am happy to report all issues were resolved and they continue to grow and prosper in their relationship. The key to their success is they learned to give up their individual need to be right and to put selfish egos on the shelf. They truly listened to each other.

People all need to be heard and feel they have been listened to by those around them. I believe it to be a basic human need. If it were not, solitary confinement would not be one of the worst punishments. Most relationship counselors would say the same.

The skills to listen and communicate effectively with each other are critical to improve your relationships, in particular with your significant other. This is the only way to keep, maintain, and grow as a couple. Quit waiting for your turn to talk. Listen carefully, and base what you say on what you hear rather than rehearsing your diatribe while they are talking so you can set them straight.

Offspring

When it comes to your children, how and when you communicate with them becomes critical. Remember, children need to communicate. Communication is how they learn, how their brain grows, and how they will eventually develop their sense of self.

The sooner you begin using adult communication skills with your toddlers, the faster they will develop strong communication skills. I have an aloe plant in my front yard that has thorns and looks like a cactus. When my grandson was four years old, I made a comment about being careful not to let the cactus stick him. He looked at me and said, adult-like, "Grandpa, it's not a cactus. It's an aloe." He certainly set me straight. Another time he looked at me as we used a hand sanitizer and said, "Look, it dissipates!" Sure enough, his parents often communicate with him using adult language and communication skills. He is now six and speaks adult—when he wants to.

As children grow, they inevitably reach the teenage years. Who among us, having lived through raising a teenager, doesn't have miscommunication stories? I'm not sure about your experience, but I found that if you do not ask the correct questions, you will not get a straight answer. Teenagers are wired to test the boundaries—it's part of the healthy process of separating from their parents and becoming people in their own right. Consequently, teenagers need to have important boundaries communicated clearly so they know what is expected and what consequences they face for overstepping. Your communication skills will either help or hinder your relationship with your teens, depending on your skill set and your ability to remain the adult in these situations. As this book explores the communication skills and mindset needed to experience more positive outcomes, be careful to not beat yourself up. I didn't know what I didn't know with regard to the skills or mindset required until I suddenly had a teenager in my very own home. I had to do some skill development quick!

Drama Queens and Kings

Often, people attempt to pull others into the drama they create in their own lives. The Karpman Drama Triangle describes this communication style where one person is the victim, one is the persecutor, and one is the enabler.

The roles can change quickly as people play out the dramas in their daily lives. At times, two people can accomplish all three roles.

It is vital to extricate yourself from these situations. All they do is drain your energy and your patience. Good communication skills are required to limit the negative consequences these games can exact from your psyche. Letting others know you are not participating in their drama is usually not easy. But, when you have a communication process and improved communication skills, you will get better outcomes.

Coworkers, Bosses, Clients/Customers

The workplace seems to be a buzz of activity and personalities. While at times you might find drama kings and queens sitting next to you at work, usually the problem is miscommunication with a board member, coworker, boss, or client that won't fall into the drama category.

You may have found yourself frustrated, whether you were the boss, the subordinate, or client, due to unclear or lack of communication. Many have felt this type of stress at work. Recently, a school teacher shared this: "If you have ever had the misfortune of having a parent complain to you, your principal, or worse yet, blasted all over social media, that you were not a good teacher, then you may need to be able to put your ego aside and listen to the parent's concerns." My hope is to help you eliminate some of the miscommunications in the workplace.

The Neighbor—Friend or Foe?

An interesting aspect about neighbors is they tend to come and go due to the increasing transient nature of today's culture. Have you ever seen news clips about feuding neighbors? On occasion, the feud culminates in violence. Wouldn't it be nice to understand the dynamics of communicating so you can achieve a more positive outcome if you ever found yourself in such a situation?

Of course, there are the neighbors who believe it is their responsibility to know everything happening in the neighborhood. How do you handle the situation when they are providing way too much information, especially when it concerns you and your family? If you think about the best relationships you ever experienced with neighbors, my guess is you communicated with them in such a way that you understood each other.

All Works in Progress

The goal of this book is to give you additional information regarding communication skills and the mindset that will move you toward more positive outcomes as you deal with all the family, friends, coworkers, customers, and neighbors in your life. You will find you are already doing many of the skills I share with you. So, as I provide the lessons that have helped me to communicate for more positive outcomes, keep in mind I am a work in progress also and do not see perfection in my near future.

Let's get to the skills.

CHAPTER 2

The Skills

Relating to People

Communication is the art and skill of how human beings relate and share information with each other regarding the external environment and their personal, internal environment. As it has been said for thousands of years, in different ways: The key to more effective and efficient communication with others is to understand them first. Who are they? What is their mindset? What is their history? What is your history

> **Alert!**
> _____
>
> Give up your need to be right, and
> put your ego on the shelf.

with them? How have they communicated with you in the past? How do they prefer to communicate?

To become more effective and efficient you must first buy into the belief that it is your responsibility to do all you can to understand the other person. If not, many of the skills I talk about will lose their power and efficacy. Let me state again: You must be willing to put your ego on the shelf and give up your need to be right. This doesn't mean you don't have opinions or you concede automatically to the wishes of others. It means you listen to understand so you can craft your message to be more effective and efficient. After all, the purpose of this book is to help you communicate for more positive outcomes.

Communication Pie

In the early 1970s, UCLA Professor Albert Mehrabian conducted studies on how people derive meaning from face-to-face communications about feelings and attitudes.[*] The results are reflected in the pie chart. This basic information is critical if you are to relate to others and improve your understanding of the messages you communicate.

One of my fears in this age of technology is that people dilute 93% of a message's meaning when it is sent via text or email. I don't care how many happy faces you add to the end of a text or email. Happy faces and emojis are not able to replace the exchange when two or more human beings communicate face to face.

Communication Pie

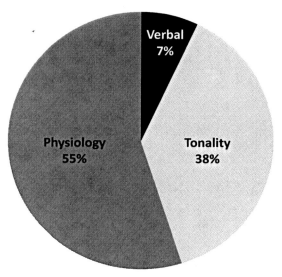

Physiology 55%

Verbal 7%

Tonality 38%

---

[*] Mehrabian, Albert, *Silent Messages,* 1971.

Physiology

How many people listen with their eyes? Based on the communication pie on the prior page, 55% of a message's meaning in a face-to-face conversation is derived from facial expressions and gestures. I bet you have noticed when people glance at their watch and look like they are ready to go. Did you acknowledge it or simply talk faster? The choice you make in such situations will either lead to a more meaningful exchange of information (perhaps later) or it will contribute to someone shutting down and not listening any further to what you say. The lesson here is to pay attention to the other person's physiology. Listen with your eyes, acknowledge what you see, and adjust your communication accordingly.

Recent research out of Ohio State University has found a specific spot in the brain that responds to people's faces and expressions.[*] This area of the brain is named the posterior superior temporal sulcus (pSTS) and is so specific and nuanced that the researchers know the facial expression the subject is observing based on the electrical stimulation pattern emitted by the pSTS. Wow! I have always told

---

[*]   Gorder, Pam Frost, "Researchers pinpoint part of the brain that recognizes facial expressions," *Ohio State News*, April 19, 2016.

salespeople and others in my sessions that they are excellent at reading people's faces. Trust your brain. It notices nuances of which you are not consciously aware.

Some people believe physiology plays an even greater role in the meaning of your communication. Deborah Bull, writer, presenter, and broadcaster and creative director of the Royal Opera House, London, writes, "Body language is a very powerful tool. We had body language before we had speech, and apparently, 80% of what you understand in a conversation is read through the body, not the words."

Tonality

It's not what you say, it's how you say it. Everyone has most likely heard this old adage when it comes to communicating with others. That saying can actually be broken down into a numerical value. Based on my experience with my own clients, I can confirm that your tonality, the sounds coming out of your mouth, contributes 38% of your message's meaning. This means 38% of how the listener interprets your message lies in the subtle nuances of how you say what you say. As you absentmindedly check your smart phone for emails or tweets and respond with a tonality implying you are not paying attention to what the other person is saying, it can result in the "sure, whatever" response. When you respond verbally in such a manner, it is usually in an "I don't care" tonality. This could be an appropriate response if you don't want to continue a conversation, but it's not good if you want to continue communicating.

Listening with your ears to what you hear and what you say is a vital skill if you want to communicate for more positive outcomes. I will spend more time on listening skills later.

Words

Words only account for 7% of your message's meaning. Yet it seems most people are more concerned about words than how they say the words and the physiology they use to deliver the words. Words are important to say what you want to say. Words become even more important when you develop the skill of listening to the words others use so you can gain insight into how better to communicate effectively with them.

> ## Alert!
>
> 93% of the meaning is in your body language and your tonality.

Here is a simple rule to remember: If your physiology, tonality, and words are incongruent with each other, you are sending a mixed message. If so, miscommunication is certain.

VAK

Let's continue this journey of understanding by realizing that each person processes and communicates information differently. What a big "aha" moment it was for me when I realized not everyone thought the same way as I did. Much like the three dominant senses (sight, sound, and touch), people tend to process the world visually, aurally, or kinesthetically. Let's explore each modality further.

Visual Modality

Visual people tend to process the world as if there is a movie running through their brain and they can see it flowing through their mind's eye. When they communicate what their brain is processing, they tend to speak quickly. After all, a picture is worth a thousand words. Visual people want to get all the words out so you can "see" what they are thinking. Many times, this will affect the grammar and enunciation of their words. Run-on sentences are also quite common. For any English teachers reading this, please be patient with a visual who is on a roll!

Visual people will tend to be animated with a lot of facial expressions and sweeping gestures. They prefer that you show them what you mean. They want to envision a solution. Sometimes they want to look at the issue from all sides. Notice how they use visual words and descriptions. And, yes, they will say they "see" what you are saying. Your words will transform into pictures in their mind. If you are unable to help them focus and see what you are attempting to communicate, the conversation will often go in circles with neither of you coming away with a clear understanding.

Auditory Modality

A person who processes aurally is referred to as an auditory. An auditory person will process the world based on words and sounds. Before words come out of an auditory person's lips, they bounce between their ears and cause them to speak slower than a visual person. An auditory person tends to speak at a normal pace and pays attention to choosing the right words to convey the correct meaning for what they are thinking and wanting to communicate with you. You can expect correct grammar, pronunciation, and enunciation. The person who constantly corrects another's grammar and pronunciation is generally in auditory modality—or is an English teacher. (Which, in my case, is also one of my sisters.)

Sound is important to auditory people, and unexpected sounds can distract from the conversation with them. After all, they want to correctly hear what you say. An auditory person expects you to tell them what you mean. They want to listen to what you say. Pay attention to the words auditory people use when they communicate with you. How something sounds or the sounds around an auditory person make a difference. While soft, consistent background noise can be soothing to auditory people, you want to avoid loud or unexpected sounds that will distract them from the conversation.

Kinesthetic Modality

The sense of touch is related to feeling. As such, a person who is in a feeling modality to process the world is referred to as a kinesthetic person. Have you ever heard the term "gut feeling"? Well, kinesthetic people process by getting a feel for what they want to communicate. So, before something comes out of their lips, it rolls around their "gut" to make sure it conveys the right sense of what they want to communicate. You guessed it! A kinesthetic person tends to talk slowly, especially when compared to a visual person.

When in kinesthetic modality, people tend to appear laid-back and relaxed. Speaking slowly, they want to be sure you get the feel of the conversation or they want you to help them get a grip on the situation. When people ask you to get a handle on the situation, they are most likely processing kinesthetically.

Observe and Identify

While everyone possesses the ability to process the world in any of the modalities, people usually prefer one over the others. However, it does not mean those people are unable to shift into the other modalities. The skill is to observe and identify the current modality of the people with whom you are communicating, and then adapt your physiology, tonality, and words to be more like them.

> ## Alert!
> ──────────────────────
> People process information differently!

Behavioral Styles

Human beings have observed each other for centuries. Through this observation, four distinct behavioral styles have come to be defined. Each style has unique characteristics and preferences in interacting with others. When you pay attention to how other people are behaving, you can glean clues that will help you communicate more effectively.

The skill is more than just observing the other person's behavior and then adjusting your communication with them. It includes the ability to think on your feet and be self-aware enough to make the adjustments. Part of the challenge is that there are few people who behave exclusively in any one of the styles. Only 2% of the population would be considered exclusive to any of the four styles.

I have seen many behavioral style assessments over the years, but they all have the same basic four styles. Let's start with an understanding of the four behavioral styles as defined by DISC: Dominant, Influencer, Steady Relator, and Compliant. Different assessments may use different names for the styles, but the characteristics are the same.

Dominant

Someone who is predominantly a Dominant is referred to as a High-D. High-D individuals are said to be task focused and want to get things done, the quicker the better. Two of the most important things to a High-D are power and control. A High-D who feels a loss of control in a conversation will often communicate in a way that will cause the other person to feel intimidated. When High-Ds are under pressure, they tend to appear insensitive.

High-Ds are not chit-chatters because they are results oriented and will get frustrated if they feel the conversation is wasting time. They want to get right to the point. Being strong-willed, competitive, and big-picture oriented, listening is not their strength.

Skills to develop when communicating with High-Ds are to make sure you are brief, to the point, big picture, results oriented, and non-emotional, and don't out-dominate them. This doesn't mean to tuck tail and let them run roughshod over you. It is OK to stand your ground, but do it in a way that identifies opportunity, is logical, and gives them a feeling they are winning.

High-Ds make quick decisions, and they have no problem telling you what they think and feel. Humility is not a strong characteristic. They are certain they are correct and will argue their position at great length. When presented with logic, limited facts, and results, High-Ds can be swayed.

Alert!

There is no "bad" behavioral style—just different.

While I am not a pure High-D, I have enough to exhibit many of the Dominant characteristics. One of my mottos has been, "I will argue my position as if it is the Holy Grail—until I am proven wrong. Then I will argue my new position as passionately as the previous position." Of course, communicating with such a motto has not always served me well. Come to think of it, exhibiting such behavior has mostly caused problems. Over time I have adjusted to do more listening and less telling, resulting in improved relationships.

Influencer

Someone who is predominantly an Influencer is called a High-I. High-Is like to connect with people and feelings. High-Is like recognition and will seek attention in order to get it. Rejection from others is one of their biggest fears. Beware, High-Is tend to overpromise and under deliver. They think they can get it all done but spend so much time socializing that the task suffers.

Be prepared to spend time chatting with High-Is. They like fast and friendly banter, but not the cutting kind. If you put them down or make them appear foolish with your quips, they are unsure if it was banter or real. If they believe the slight to be real, their fear is you might not like them. High-Is want to be liked.

When communicating with a High-I, lighten up and have fun. Use touch on the forearm or shoulder (if appropriate given the context) as you exhibit patience, and explore the High-I's feelings and opinions. Be warm and friendly as you listen to High-Is speak. Do not ignore them. If you happen to be a High-I, be aware you and the other High-I will want time to be heard. To be more effective, let the other go first. Put your ego on the shelf; your goal is to understand them first. Then you can communicate for more effective outcomes.

Since very few people are a pure style, I find I am a mix of Dominant and Influencer. I recall the time my Dominant style asked a businesswoman why she didn't want to work with me. She said she didn't trust me because I smiled too much. What I perceived as a strength of having a lot of High-I in me turned into a weakness. Thank heavens my Dominant asked the question so I could adjust my Influencer in the future.

Steady Relator

A Steady Relator, referred to as a High-S, likes to be around familiar people and to be part of a team, like family.

High-Ss will actively seek appreciation and acceptance. They like situations and people to remain the same. Peace and harmony is the High-S motto. Change for change's sake makes High-Ss uncomfortable. Don't expect them to rock the boat; if it is not broken, there is no need to fix it. High-Ss are very steady and patient but are too willing to sublimate what they want to get consensus and peace within the group.

When communicating with a High-S, be sure to keep your High-D impatience in check. Many times, High-Ss are bouncing situations or ideas off you to get your input to make sure what they are considering will not disrupt the group/family or effect their acceptance within the group/family.

Often High-Ss will not share how they are truly feeling for fear of not being accepted. Do your best to be patient, to listen, and to confirm what you think they might be feeling. This skill will give them a sense of being listened to and taken seriously. When High-Ss believe they are recognized, accepted, and heard, your communication with them will result in more positive outcomes.

Compliant

A Compliant style is referred to as a High-C, although some behavioral style assessments refer to them as analytical. The two most important things to High-Cs are to be right and to be perfect. They usually are both. High-Cs want to make one decision—the right one. There is no such thing as too much data for a High-C. High-Cs need the details and will analyze everything one more time so they can be sure—and will analyze again as a double check.

High-Cs tend to be overly critical and expect you to say exactly what you mean. Relationship building is not a strong suit for them, and nurturing is a foreign concept. The use of humor is not particularly effective with High-Cs. If they have a sense of humor at all, it is so dry that the rest of us usually don't get it.

As you communicate with High-Cs, stick to the facts and provide as much information as you are able. They tend to like specifics, so avoid vague, sweeping generalizations. If you must criticize their behaviors or tasks, be sure to do it in a manner that does not surprise them and only reflects criticism of the work, not them.

High-Cs will be quiet and not express emotions and will get uncomfortable if others do. Give them time to think and process your questions. After all, they want to give you the right answer. Do not pressure them and expect a quick decision.

Each Style Has a Place

Remember, there is no wrong behavioral style. The keys to improving the outcomes of your conversations are to be self-aware of your style and its strengths and weaknesses and to observe the other person to identify their style so you can adjust accordingly. To improve communication outcomes, adapt your behavioral style to be more like the person with whom you are communicating. The charts below will give you some communication clues at a glance.

HOW TO IDENTIFY

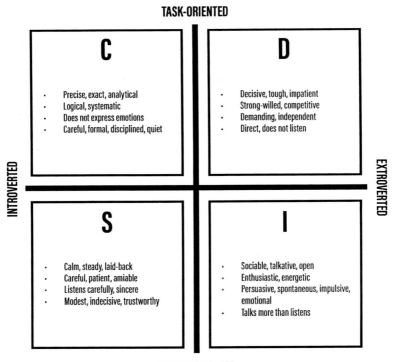

TASK-ORIENTED

C
- Precise, exact, analytical
- Logical, systematic
- Does not express emotions
- Careful, formal, disciplined, quiet

D
- Decisive, tough, impatient
- Strong-willed, competitive
- Demanding, independent
- Direct, does not listen

INTROVERTED

EXTROVERTED

S
- Calm, steady, laid-back
- Careful, patient, amiable
- Listens carefully, sincere
- Modest, indecisive, trustworthy

I
- Sociable, talkative, open
- Enthusiastic, energetic
- Persuasive, spontaneous, impulsive, emotional
- Talks more than listens

PEOPLE-ORIENTED

HOW TO COMMUNICATE

TASK-ORIENTED

INTROVERTED

C

- Use data and facts
- Examine an argument thoroughly
- Keep on task; do not socialize
- Disagree with the facts, not the person
- Use proven ideas and data
- Don't touch
- Don't talk about personal issues
- Explain carefully

D

- Be direct, brief, and to the point
- Focus on the task
- Use a results-oriented approach
- Ensure they win
- Use a logical approach
- Touch on high points and big ideas
- Don't touch; keep your distance
- Don't be emotional
- Act quickly; they decide fast

EXTROVERTED

S

- Be patient, build trust
- Draw out their opinions
- Relax; allow time for discussions
- Show how solutions affect people
- Clearly define all areas
- Involve them in planning
- Slow down your presentation
- Provide information needed
- Secure commitment step-by-step

I

- Allow time for socialization
- Lighten up; have fun
- Ask for feelings and opinions
- Use touch, if appropriate
- Be friendly and warm
- Set aside time for chatting
- Let them speak
- Give recognition
- Speak about people and feelings

PEOPLE-ORIENTED

DO'S AND DON'TS

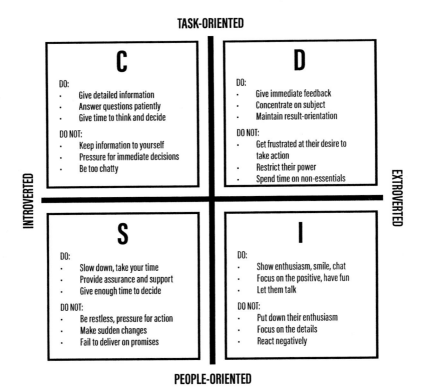

Transactional Analysis

A psychological theory that makes a lot of sense to me is transactional analysis (TA). This theory explains how and why people communicate with each other in the ways they do. Dr. Eric Berne (1910–1970) is the father of TA, and his disciples have expanded and kept TA alive and active over the years. In the next few pages, I will give you an overview of some of the basics and why TA is important if you are to have more effective and efficient outcomes in your conversations.

Dr. Berne believed human beings interact with each other from one of three ego states. At any given moment, people are using their Parent ego state, Adult ego state, or Child ego state when communicating with each other. I will explore each one and give you the highlights.

Parent

When you are a newborn and until you are about six years old, your brain is recording all the do's and don'ts of life: the rules. Most of us learn these rules of life from parents; hence the name Parent ego state as the recorder of all this information.

"Look both ways before crossing the _____!"

Most of you can fill in the blank with the word "street" without thinking. You recorded the "crossing the street" rule within your Parent ego state as a child. The theory is that this information, recorded when you were young, now whizzes through your brain in an endless loop ready in an instant to burst forth from your lips. Your inner

Parent records the rules, judgments, and eventually the beliefs you experienced as you grew up. So, whenever you are expressing judgments, beliefs, or citing rules, you are in your Parent ego state.

You also record how others respond to you as you follow the rules—or you don't. This is important because whatever behavior you observe as people react to you is also recorded and available for use later in life. As an example, a child might not actually look both ways before crossing the street. The parent seeing this then proceeds to chastise the child with, "What's wrong with you? How many times do I have to tell you to look both ways? You can't leave the yard for a month!" This is an example of a parent modeling Critical Parent.

Anytime you hear yourself saying or catch yourself thinking, "You should...," "You ought...," "You must...," you are in the Critical Parent ego state. Likewise, you are in the Critical Parent ego state if you catch yourself saying or thinking, "What's wrong with you? Why can't you? Don't you know better?" Most people do not respond well when you communicate to them with Critical Parent messages. Don't worry! There is an alternative.

You might catch yourself seeking to further understand someone else or empathizing with them. If so, you are in the

Nurturing Parent ego state. Whenever you provide comfort, a shoulder to cry on, or an understanding ear, you are expressing your Nurturing Parent. It is the Nurturing Parent model you recorded when life wasn't going so well when you were a little tyke. It is the Nurturing Parent ego state that allows you to replay nurturing behavior when others around you have had misfortune or been hurt.

The interesting consequence of what you recorded as a youngster is you have a bit of both—Critical and Nurturing Parent—available to you as you communicate with others. How it plays out is based on the situations in which you find yourself. Many times, it depends on the person with whom you are communicating.

Child

At the same time your Parent ego state is recording, you have another ego state recording all your emotional reactions to everything happening to you. This is called your Child ego state. From children's perspective, the world revolves around them. From ages zero to six, your Child recorded every "I'm happy," "I'm mad," "I'm glad," and "I'm sad" feeling you felt. It also recorded all the egocentric "I want; I need; it's all about me" feelings and thoughts. Now, as a mature adult, whenever you are feeling emotional or selfish, you are in your Child ego state.

But as you recorded these emotions, you also had a Little Professor in your head to help you figure out how to get what you wanted. Early on, children learn to repeat the behavior that is successful. If they express anger, throw tantrums, and then they get what they want, they will continue such behavior and carry it with them into adulthood. Every time you find yourself in drama king or queen mode, you are in the Rebellious Child ego state.

As adults, when someone is communicating in Rebellious Child mode, the chances of reaching mutually acceptable outcomes diminish. When both communicators in an interaction are in this ego state, the conversation will typically degenerate to the point of becoming a shouting match with all parties becoming upset.

The Little Professor in you may have recorded a different scenario. You went into your tantrum; you didn't get what you wanted; and perhaps, you angered those around you. When you adapted your raw emotional response to be more appropriate, you were rewarded with acceptance and affection. When this happened regularly, you recorded more Adaptive Child messages.

Once grown up, you may find yourself doing all you

can to please the other person and never sharing how you truly feel. This would be operating from an extreme Adaptive Child ego state. Following socially acceptable responses would be an appropriate use of your Adaptive Child ego state.

But we can't forget the Natural Child in all of us. Have you ever watched five year olds being five year olds with no adult interference? Kids figure it out. Sure, there might be some tears or conflicts, but they get beyond it and do what comes naturally. They have fun!

When you hear yourself telling a joke that is just plain silly, when you dance like no one is watching, or when you sing along with the song at the top of your lungs, you are in your Natural Child ego state. Let's all have fun, and do-overs are allowed!

Adult

Dr. Berne described one more ego state: the Adult ego state. The Adult ego state records the information. It makes no judgments and has no emotional attachments. Information in and information out is the role of the Adult ego state.

When you ask questions to gather information, you would typically be in your Adult ego state. When you share information, again it is the Adult ego state. The moment you become judgmental or emotional, you transitioned into the Critical Parent or Child ego state. This chart* will help you understand the difference.

Avoid Your Critical Parent's Judgmental Messages

JUDGMENTAL	HELPFUL
"You should…"	"You may find more value in…"
"You should have…"	"Had you considered…?"
"You shouldn't…"	"It might not help to…"
"Don't do…"	"You may want to consider…"
"You're wrong about…"	"Your perspective might change if…"
"You missed the point."	"Have you considered…?"
"You just don't get it."	"Perhaps you should think about…"
"Listen to me."	"May I suggest…?"

---

*   From Sandler Training's Sales Mastery® program.

Putting It into Practice

Why is an understanding of the three ego states important? Because they affect the quality of your communications. The skill to be learned is self-awareness of the ego state from which you are operating and to recognize which ego state the other person is using to communicate. Communicate from your Nurturing Parent and Adult ego states most of the time. This will help you avoid the games and misunderstandings which TA is so good at bringing to light.

Imagine this scenario. I walk downstairs and ask my wife, "Have you seen my car keys?" She responds as Critical Parent and replies, "If you would hang your keys on the key rack like I've told you, you wouldn't be losing them all the time! I hope you never find them!" If I respond in Rebellious Child or Critical Parent mode, the game is on and the conversation generally degenerates into something neither of us intended.

It could have sounded something like this, "Have you seen my car keys?" This time she replies from her Child ego state (emotionally), "Why do you think it is my responsibility to keep track of your car keys? I am sick and tired of picking up after you and making sure you don't lose anything." This conversation, too, can become very confrontational and emotional if I decide to respond further in my Critical Parent or my Child ego state.

Adult-to-Adult, it would sound more like this: "Have you seen my car keys?" Her reply could be, "Yes, I have. They are on the bedroom dresser." Or her reply could have been, "No, I haven't seen them." Either of those replies supplies the information requested and will not lead to a downward spiral with further conversation.

There is one more possible response: Nurturing Parent. I ask, "Have you seen my car keys?" She replies, "No, I haven't. Do you want some help looking for them?" This response makes it difficult for the conversation to go in a negative direction.

The assumption I made in all the above scenarios is I was in Adult ego state. If my tonality or physiology with my original question was incongruous with Adult ego state, it could come off as emotional Child who needs help or a Critical Parent who blamed her. Don't forget the Communication Pie and how much meaning is in the physiology and tonality.

When you feel the need to share your feelings, realize it is your Child ego state's need. Remind yourself to communicate as best you can in the Adult ego state. Do your best to report the feelings as information and not act on them. Be clear to the other person you are expressing feelings for informational input to further the conversation and understanding.

As much as I would like for you to adapt your modality and behavioral style to be more aligned with the other person, I do not think it wise to adapt to any non-productive ego states. If they are communicating from the Critical Parent or Child, it doesn't mean you should. Do your best to stay in your Adult and Nurturing Parent ego states.

Connect to the Other Person

To bond and establish rapport, it is important to connect with the other people when you communicate. An easy way to accomplish this is to ask connect questions. A connect question focuses on them, their family, their hobbies, or their career.

These types of questions are more important when you are first getting to know someone. But don't get lazy just because you know someone well. It is still a good idea to ask personal connect questions when beginning a conversation as a way of reconnecting.

Examples of connect questions would be:

- "So, what brings you to the fundraiser?"
- "How long have you lived in the neighborhood?"

- ◆ "Looks like your kid has some real skills. How long has she been playing?"
- ◆ "What keeps you busy when you're not working?"
- ◆ "I see you're wearing a Buckeyes shirt. Are you a fan?"
- ◆ "What business are you in?"

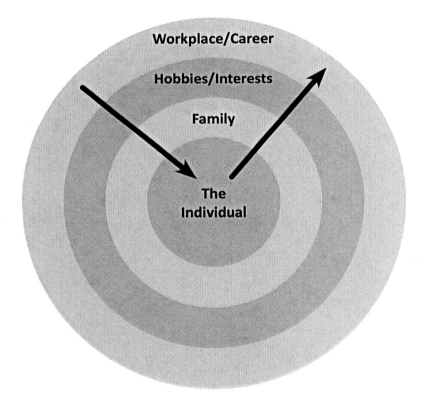

If you begin with questions to the individual and work outward as illustrated above, you can usually achieve a nice flow to the conversation. There are occasions when this approach is viewed as too personal, especially with people you have just met. In such cases, work from the outer rings in.

OK/Not-OK Theory

There is one more contribution provided by TA that I believe has a large impact on how well people communicate with others. The rule is simple: Do not cause the other person to feel Not-OK.

Psychologists (specifically Dr. Thomas Harris, in his book *I'm OK—You're OK*) believe people would rather feel good and OK rather than bad and not-OK. The problem is most people feel less than OK at any one point in time. The psychologists are not implying people are all mentally unstable. They are referring to the constant voice in people's heads, which often is giving a negative message.

You may have experienced getting up at night for a drink of water and in the darkness you stub your toe. Have you ever heard yourself think, "Idiot! I can't believe I did that." This is an example of feeling not-OK. Any time you belittle, demean, antagonize, condescend, or make fun of someone, you cause the other person to feel not-OK. When this happens to them, people immediately distance themselves or remove the source of their not OK-ness; it is a conversation ender.

If you are causing someone to feel not-OK, ask yourself whether you are feeling OK or not-OK yourself. At times, you might cause another to feel more not-OK than you. Psychologists say this is how you might get to feel more OK with yourself—by making someone else less OK than you. This would explain why so many people watch soap operas, talk shows, and news programs that feature people in not-OK situations. As you watch, you can say, "Thank heavens I don't have to experience such disaster!" Thus, you get an uptick in your feeling of being OK.

I must admit firsthand knowledge of this in action. Remember in the first paragraph of this book when I mentioned failed relationships? I recall specific situations from many years ago when the OK/Not-OK theory bit me.

I would have a particularly bad day and come home feeling not-OK. I would grouse, complain, and pick a fight. Sure, enough when my then-wife became angrier (less OK) than myself. I would respond with, "Well, if you are going to be so upset, we can talk about this later!" As I removed myself from the conversation, I felt a little more OK than I was before. Now I understand how my Critical Parent and Child ego states may have been involved in my attempt to feel more OK. Both of us would engage in this type of behavior so it is no wonder this relationship failed as we decided to remove the perceived source of our not OK-ness—each other!

Now, knowing this can happen, I work at keeping the other person OK. At times, I will be a little not-OK on purpose to ensure they are feeling OK in the conversation. It might sound like this: "My fault; I probably heard you wrong. What is it you are wanting me to do?" If you can give up your need to be right and can put your ego on the shelf, being not-OK on purpose can work well.

This chart* may help you understand what not-OK and OK mean. Let's put some meaning behind these terms.

NOT-OK	OK
Upset	Confident
Overwhelmed	Secure
Insecure	Respected
Unhappy	Satisfied
Ignored	Appreciated
Pressured	In Control

---

* From Sandler Training's Sales Mastery® program.

More Positive Outcomes

The basic skills I have shared deal with your ability to read people and understand them at a basic behavioral and psychological level. Once you understand how they are processing information, the style they prefer, and the ego state in which they are choosing to communicate, you can laser focus your questions and responses to make them feel listened to, understood, and OK. When you accomplish that, you will communicate for more positive outcomes.

Alert!

When you communicate with other people in a manner that reflects the modality in which they are processing information and the behavioral style they are most like, while you stay in your Nurturing Parent and Adult ego states, you will keep them feeling OK and you will tend to get more positive outcomes.

CHAPTER 3

The Art of Mutual Agreements

Starting the Conversation

I remember taking a parenting class when my boys were young. The big takeaways from the class were the requirement to tell your child what the consequences of their behavior would be and to be clear on what you expected from them. I recall my boys' mother and me saying to each other on numerous occasions, "We can't get mad at them if we weren't clear with our expectations."

Sometimes, it sounded like, "Don't punish them if you didn't tell them they would be punished."

When my sons were teenagers, I became involved with training salespeople. Three rules* jumped out at me because they are so eloquent in their simplicity.

- First, people don't get mad at you when you tell them what you are going to do and they agree to it.
- Second, you shouldn't get mad at someone for doing something you didn't tell them they couldn't do.
- Third, no "mutual mystification."** Make sure all parties to the conversation have a clear understanding of what was said and what is going to happen next.

Basically, these were the same strategies I learned in the parenting class. When you start a conversation, get agreements up front about what you and the other person want to happen and what you don't want to happen as you talk; then, confirm what you both decided.

When you find yourself in a conversation with someone who did something you didn't want them to do, ask yourself this, "When did I tell them I didn't want them to do

---

*   Source: Sandler Training.
**   *The Sandler Rules*, #3.

that?" The follow-up question is, "If I did tell them, when did they agree not to do it?"

Let's spend some time on the key things you need to get agreement on when starting a conversation. When I say "conversation," I am not talking about the chitchat or banter that people often engage in with each other. Conversation in this context means a purposeful interaction between people to persuade or exchange required information essential in decision making.

Did you catch the clarification above as an example of no mutual mystification? Are you clear on the type of conversations we are now discussing?

Purpose

All participants in the conversation need to have a clear understanding of its purpose. If you and your spouse want to have a conversation about planning your next Hawaiian vacation, make sure you both agree to discuss the planning. If the conversation is more serious, such as deciding how to discipline the kids, be crystal clear on why you are having the conversation. If you want to have a conversation with your teenagers or your teenagers want to have a conversation with you about curfews, be sure you all know this is the purpose. Stick to the purpose of the conversation. Do your best not to get sidetracked on other issues unrelated to your stated and agreed-upon purpose.

Don't forget that your Nurturing Parent ego state can help set the stage. "Thanks for taking the time to plan our trip to Hawaii with me," sounds much better than, "Sit your butt down and help me plan this Hawaii trip!" How you open the conversation can set the tone for what is to come.

When setting the purpose of the conversation, there is no wrong purpose. You have the right to discuss whatever you feel the two (or more) of you need to discuss. The strategy is to make sure you all agree to the purpose of the conversation before you jump into the conversation. This will ensure no one is surprised.

Few things are worse than hearing, "We need to talk," or "Do you have time to talk?" Add what it is you want to talk about immediately so the other person can determine if now, or later, is a better time to discuss the topic. A better way to begin could be, "We need to talk about..." Providing a subject is a clue to the purpose of the conversation.

Time

The next item to be very clear about is the amount of time required or requested. Conversations have a way of expanding or contracting to fill the amount of time given. If no specific duration is agreed upon, a conversation can drag on for what seems like an eternity. When you let people know how much time you need of their undivided attention, they are more apt to give it to you. You must make sure your time request is reasonable. If the other person feels that you are asking for more time than is reasonable or more than they are willing to give, there is a good chance they will decline or, if they agree, they will not be totally focused.

It is OK to schedule a time to discuss a topic. It could sound like this: "Do you have 15 minutes to start planning our trip to Hawaii?" Notice that this combines the purpose with the request for time. If the answer is "yes," go forward with your discussion. If the answer is "no," simply ask, "When can we schedule 15 minutes so we can start planning?" If you need 30 minutes, ask for 30 minutes. Schedule the time and have the conversation as planned.

When the scheduled time arrives, start the conversation with nurturing. "Thanks for taking the time to work on a plan for our trip to Hawaii. Are you still good for the 15 minutes?" Confirm the time in case something may have changed. It shows you respect the other person's time. Be prepared to end the conversation in 15 minutes.

If you need to schedule more time, do so and continue the conversation later. Agreement on the amount of time is crucial.

Carefully choose the time to have your conversation depending on the purpose or topic. The more serious or potentially emotional the conversation, the more reason to choose or schedule a time when both are rested and relaxed. A tough conversation after a not-OK day at work is a recipe for disaster.

A final thought on time. For the important conversations, do your best to schedule uninterrupted time. Turn off smart phones, televisions, and computers (unless you need one of these tools to gather information during your discussion).

Their Expectations

In the beginning of your conversations, be sure to discover the important or key areas the other people are expecting to cover. Remember, your goal is to understand them first, which will allow you to better focus the exchange.

When you understand what they want to talk about or their key issues regarding the topics, you will get a clue as to how to proceed. If the issues they prefer to discuss are not the same as yours, it is OK. At this point, you only want to uncover their topics. There is no wrong agenda or expectations for them to have regarding the conversation. Once they share their concerns, review to be sure there is mutual agreement concerning their expectations.

It might sound like this:

You: "Thanks for taking the time to chat about our vacation to Hawaii. I know we decided yesterday to start this process today. Are you still OK with the 30 minutes we planned for today?"

Other: "Sure, now is a good time."

You: "Great, I'll turn off my cell phone so we don't get interrupted."

Other: "Makes sense; so will I."

You: "So what are the key areas you think we should focus on?"

Other: "Let's start with airfare and times."

You: "OK. So if we get through the airfares and times to depart and arrive, that would be a good start?"

Other: "Oh yeah, a great start."

What has happened, in the above idealistic conversation, is that you have involved them, which allows them to feel ownership of the trip and the planning. Did you notice how I also included purpose and duration in the dialog? You also confirmed, via mutual agreement, what they consider to be important. Beware of your Critical Parent ego state when you want to tell them how off-base they are for not choosing the issues you think are more important. Stay in your Adult ego state and acknowledge their right to have an opinion.

Your Expectations

Now is the time for you to get your expectations on the table. Both parties will benefit by knowing each other's expectations. It could sound like this: "It makes sense to get the dates and airfare squared away, but I also want to make sure we spend some time deciding on a hotel."

If you want to discuss different aspects of the topic other than what the other person came up with, the beginning of the conversation is the time to let them know your desire to explore additional related issues. It wouldn't make sense if you want to talk about buying a new car if the purpose of the conversation is to plan the vacation. Or would it? What if buying a new car affects the budget for the vacation? Now it becomes a related topic. All conversational strategies are situational. What to include or leave out is determined by the actual context in which the conversation occurs.

A major expectation, which is always a positive, is an increased understanding of the other person. To accomplish understanding, there is a good chance you will need to ask questions. Get permission to ask questions. It could be as simple as this: "Just to make sure I don't get confused, is it OK if I ask questions as we go along?"

Outcomes

At the end of your conversation, what are the possible outcomes? What decisions will need to be made? Conversations will be more productive and achieve more positive outcomes when you know in advance what options are available. The outcomes fall into one of two categories: *yes* or *no*.

A *yes* and a *no* can have many different meanings. A *yes* can mean that a conflict has been resolved, that information has been exchanged, or that you and the other person agree to continue the conversation.

In the previous example, it could sound like this: "So, at the end of our 30-minute planning session, we should be able to nail down our flights, decide which hotel, and have a good idea of what needs to be done next. Make sense to you?"

> ## Alert!
>
> ---
>
> Mutual agreements are not "one and done." They should be occurring throughout the entire conversation.

The Five Key Components: PLATE

An easy way to remember the five key components of getting the conversation starts with the mnemonic PLATE.[*] Think of it this way. To have a civilized dinner, you first put the food on the plate. The same is true for a civilized conversation. Get the mutual agreements on the PLATE, up front, before you get started.

- ◆ **Purpose.** Letting the other person know why you want to have the conversation is required. You can't wait until time runs out and surprise them with a purpose of which they knew nothing. Remember,

---

[*]   Source: Sandler Training.

no mutual mystification. Be up front with why you want to engage in the conversation.

* **Limit the time.** You must agree on the time limit of the conversation and live up to that agreement. If you need more time, set another mutual agreement as to how much more time is needed, when you will continue, and what else needs to be discussed. You could also have agreed to more time in the beginning.

* **Agenda of their expectations.** Discover what is important to them first. Even though it may be your desire to have the conversation, allow them to go first. Once you know what is important to them, you might decide to alter your approach.

* **Topics.** Let the other person know your expectations of what you want to discuss or not to discuss. Always get permission to ask questions so you can understand what is important to them. Get the truth on the table. Let them know exactly what you want to talk about and what you will be doing during the conversation, like asking questions. If both understand the concepts of the Parent, Adult, and Child ego states, I like to add this question: "Can we do our best to stay in the Adult ego state?" Tough

conversations make it very easy to slip into Critical Parent or Rebellious Child ego states.

◆ **E̲ventual goal.** Share what you hope the outcome of the conversation will be. Perhaps it is resolution to a problem or agreement on a plan of action. The point is to have a goal to go for in the conversation defined up front, in the beginning of the conversation. This will certainly help keep you on topic.

Mutual Agreement

If for some reason the current conversation needs to be continued in the future, mutual agreements still apply. To start the next conversation properly, the end of this conversation should have a mutual agreement about the purpose, timing, expectations, and probable outcomes of the next conversation.

The art of mutual agreements is not a one-and-done deal. Mutual up-front agreements are obvious ones, but don't forget to formulate mutual agreements as needed throughout the conversation as both parties agree to concepts, duties, responsibilities, and compromises. You also need to agree if there is another conversation needed for a resolution regarding the issue being discussed.

CHAPTER 4

Questions

The Pitfalls of Asking Questions

Those of us who experienced raising children are familiar with the exasperation of too many questions. Anyone with a two-year-old can tell you how frustrating it becomes to hear the 75th "why" of the hour. But for a two-year-old, this is how they learn—by asking questions.

If the person with whom you are having a conversation feels as if you are an IRS audit agent or a police interrogator, you are evasive, or you ask questions just to ask questions, the outcome will not be good. The other person will shut down and become uncommunicative. Those types of questions are what I call "brick" questions.

Nurture versus Inquisition

A brick question usually comes from your Critical Parent ego state and feels like you are smacking the other person for not doing what you want them to do. Leading into a conversation with your teenager with a brick question like, "Why are you coming home so late?," increases the odds the teenager will become defensive and may become uncooperative. I suggest you begin with a nurturing comment like, "It worries me when you're not in by your curfew. I fear something has happened to you. What caused you to miss your curfew?"

When you become an empathetic Nurturing Parent, you have an improved chance of having a meaningful conversation. In addition, when you question with "what caused you to" versus "why did you," you are redirecting the conversation away from an attack on the person and more toward discovering the real issue. Once you uncover the real issue, it is easier to solve the problem. Nurturing Parent does not mean to become a pushover. It means you deliver your message and any consequences in an under-standing and nurturing manner.

In the previous example, you may discover your teenager chose to ignore the up-front agreement for curfew. Notice how I gave you the benefit of the doubt? I assumed you had a previous conversation about a curfew and the two of you came to some mutual agreements about time and con-sequence. Previous mutual agreements with others make future conversations go more smoothly and reach more positive outcomes.

If the other person is not living up to a previous agree-ment, it is OK to be "nurturingly" assertive with your questions to find out why and to follow through on the consequences. The first time you fail to follow through with agreed-upon consequences, all future agreements become suspect.

Not Listening to Answers

I am guilty! I can't tell you how many times I have asked someone a question and not listened to their answer. They start to answer, and, as soon as I hear a key word, I jump in with my assumptions of what the answer is going to be. On many occasions, I have been wrong.

What I have learned is to pay attention. That means to

take the time to really listen to what their answer is before responding. If you are asking questions, give them time to answer fully. It does no good to ask questions if you are not willing and able to listen to the answers.

If you ask a question and then continue with your diatribe without considering their answer, you risk making them feel not-OK and uncomfortable with continuing the conversation. Remember, people want to feel they have been heard. Take the time to acknowledge their answer through active listening (more on that subject later), and consider how their answer will affect what you say next.

Not Waiting for Answers

Another pitfall of asking questions is closely related to not listening to answers. When you ask questions without waiting for others to answer, you might as well tell them that what they are saying is not important to you. With such a frame of mind, it is difficult to achieve positive outcomes.

One reason people do not allow for enough time for the other person to answer is they might be uncomfortable with silence. I urge you to give people time to process your question and to formulate an answer. It will make a difference.

I learned this back in my college years. I had to do a

senior communication project. Since I was working part-time at the local utility company delivering mail to the executives, it made sense to craft a project based on my workplace. So, I crafted the project and set a time with the CEO to present it and gain his approval.

The weekend before my big presentation, I found myself reading a newspaper article on sales. Being a college student, this was not my usual practice. In the article, it said, "Whenever you ask a closing question, shut up. Whoever speaks next loses. If it is you, you will buy their stalls and objections. If it is them, they will buy your product or service." To this day, I have no idea why this quote was emblazoned into my brain. I have heard many versions of it since.

The day of the presentation came. I found myself in this wood-paneled office with the CEO in his power suit and tie. I mustered all my intestinal fortitude, made my presentation, and asked, "Will you allow me to use you and your executives for my project?" I immediately looked down and watched my shoes for about ten seconds.

When I looked up, he was pondering my project. He was rubbing his chin, rubbing his forehead, and putting his reading glasses off and on as he pondered. There was a clock over his left shoulder. As he pondered, I watched the clock. Nearly four minutes went by! Do you have any idea how long four minutes can seem?

He finally looked at me and said, "Young man, you read the newspaper!"

I responded with, "Does that mean I can use your team for my project?"

He laughed and said, "Of course, you can. I was just testing you. But I have another meeting and I am out of time."

What a lesson to learn. Over the years, I have morphed the initial quote into a simple rule: Whenever you ask any question, shut up. Give them time to answer!

Getting Emotional

When the answer to your question is not what you were hoping to hear, you might react by becoming emotional. Your emotional Child ego state gets involved, and you might respond with something to make it all about you or get your feelings hurt and blame the other person. It is OK to have feelings, but you must be careful to avoid the emotional outburst.

If you are emotional when you ask a question, it will skew what you ask, how you ask it, and the way you interpret the answer. Asking a question emotionally—"Why do you always upset me by coming in late?"—practically begs other people to respond in Critical Parent or Rebellious Child.

- The Critical Parent would respond with, "What's wrong with you? Everything I say or do seems to upset you. What's your problem?"
- The Rebellious Child could respond with, "Why do you always think it's my fault because you keep getting upset? I am sick and tired of you blaming me for your problems!"

Neither of these responses are conducive to a productive conversation. My suggestion is to ask your question differently. "I feel upset every time you come in late. Why do you think I feel that way?" This reframing of the question will allow the other person to explore the reasons you are feeling upset. It could be because you are worried or unable to sleep until they get home. The point here is to phrase the questions so you own your feelings without blaming them.

When the reasons are uncovered, perhaps a mutual agreement can be reached to alleviate your feeling upset. Your loved ones can agree to call if they know they are going to be late. The conversation then goes in a different direction with a much-preferred outcome.

Questioning Strategies and Techniques

There are many reasons to ask questions, and there are many ways to ask questions. You could ask to obtain information. Perhaps you ask to clarify understanding. You might even ask to make sure that other people feel they were heard.

In this next section, I will explore the types of questions to ask, the reasons to ask, and how to ask. These are presented in no particular order, and please do not feel you must use all of them in every conversation. You might discover you use many of these questioning strategies and techniques already. This section will be giving names to the types of questions.

Alert!

You will not use each of these techniques
in every conversation you have. They
are to be used appropriately.

Awareness Questions

Many times, people are not aware of how they are impacting others. If it is in a negative manner, wouldn't you appreciate knowing this so you can adjust if appropriate? If you knew you affected others in a positive manner, knowing that would give an uptick in your OK-ness. Use awareness questions to help other people become aware of the impact they are having.

You want to use these questions to expand the awareness of someone, but be careful. How you phrase these questions can make all the difference in outcomes. Saying to someone, "Don't you know you seem to have a bad impact on Robert?," or "You know you make people mad when you say these things, don't you?," sounds harsh and comes off as a Critical Parent.

The whole point of an awareness question is to explore if the others realize how their conversation affects other people. Soften what you say by using negatively phrased questions. An example is, "You probably don't realize the negative impact you had on Robert, do you?" This question allows you to discover other people's level of self-awareness.

If the answer is "yes," meaning they were aware, you can shift your questions to discover if the negative impact was intentional or unintentional. The answer will dictate where the conversation goes from there. If the answer is "no," you can provide feedback as to why what was said, how it was said, and the words spoken might have a negative impact.

Anytime you can expand people's self-awareness in regards to how their communication style affects others, you are helping them grow and become more effective and efficient communicators. But you must communicate this from Nurturing Parent and Adult ego states while keeping them feeling OK with you. Be sure to be aware of your physiology and tonality. It makes a difference and is not always an easy task.

When my kids were young, I coached them in athletics. I attended the National Youth Sports Coaches Association classes on coaching youngsters and on the sport that I coached. As a coach, I met many of the parents and interacted with them in the community as well as on the field.

Years later I had an opportunity to reacquaint myself with Pat, one of those parents. Pat and I got to know each other much better all these years later, and I found out what a great guy he is. Pat shared something with me that made a huge impact on my self-awareness of how I communicated with others.

Pat told me I was intimidating and unapproachable back in the years when our boys were on the same team. He said he didn't realize I was such a fun, easygoing guy. Reflecting, I think his assessment was correct. It took me years of learning and maturity to put my ego on the shelf and to give up my need to be right. According to Pat, it made communicating with me more enjoyable. Thanks, Pat!

Another type of awareness question occurs in the beginning of the conversation. When you say to someone, "I need to talk with you about why I am not comfortable with another dog in the house. Is now a good time to discuss it?," you are making them aware of the topic of discussion. This fits well with the up-front agreement I mentioned earlier. Make the other person aware of your issue, how much time it will take, and the possible outcomes. If you need to go back and reread the mutual-agreement pages, you will find the questions that you ask by using the PLATE model fall into the awareness questions category.

So, awareness questions fall into one of two large categories. First, there are questions to discern the level of self-awareness the other person has about how their communication affects others. Second, there are questions to make sure the other person is aware of the issues/topics, the time requested, and the expected outcomes.

Engagement Questions

No, I am not talking about the "Will you marry me?" question! (But that really is the ultimate engagement question you can ask.)

In many conversations, you attempt to get other people to do something you want them to do or to help you do something you want to do. You need to figure out whether or not they are willing and able to engage, which means they're spending the time, money, resources, or energy required. Sometimes a person is willing to help but is not able to invest the time, money, resources, or energy. On other occasions, the other person is able invest the time, money, resources, or energy required but might not be willing to do so.

An engagement question should discover if the other person is willing and able to engage in doing what you are asking. If not, it is OK to ask questions to find out why. A built-in assumption is that you have already made clear what would be required.

It might sound like this: "Jason, I am donating my old propane grill to the church. It will take me about an hour tomorrow between 9 and 10 A.M. to load it, drop it off at the church, and get back home. Will you let me use your pick-up truck and help me load it?" The answer will let you know if Jason is willing and able to engage in your request. See, I told you that you were already asking these types of questions. Now it has a name!

Alert!

To determine the other person's willingness and ability to engage with you, you must ask engagement questions.

Most people will tell you why they are unable or unwilling to help. If you feel the need to probe further as to their reasons, remember to be in Nurturing Parent or Adult ego states as you ask further questions. In the Adult ego state, it might sound like this: "Sounds like tomorrow is not good for you. Would you be available another time, or should I ask someone else?"

Scope-and-Significance Questions

Not only will you be asking others to do things or to help you, but they will also be asking you to do what they want you to do. It is important to have a clear understanding of what it is they are asking of you. Scope-and-significance questions are asked to clarify their request of your time, money, resources, or energy. There is nothing fancy or unusual in asking these types of questions. The questions should be simple, like the following examples.

- ◆ "How much time will it require?"
- ◆ "How much money will it cost me?"
- ◆ "When does it need to happen?"
- ◆ "How long will you need my vehicle?"
- ◆ "Will anyone else be helping us?"
- ◆ "How important is this to you?"

You get the idea of how to ask a scope-and-significance question. You can ask the questions in an appropriate manner and use the words that clearly get the information you need to make your decision. Because you are requesting information, do your best to stay in your Adult ego state as the discussion continues. Please notice the similarity of scope-and-significance questions to the next type of questions, which are impact questions.

Impact Questions

You would ask this type of question to do your best to understand the impact that the conversation or resulting outcomes will have on other people. After you learn how they will be impacted, ask questions to be sure they understand how you will be impacted. Impacts fall into two categories: positive impacts or negative impacts. Knowing how each of you is impacted can make a huge difference as to whether or not the conversation ends with a positive outcome. Yes, you can achieve a positive outcome even when the impact on either of you is negative.

Remember the Hawaiian vacation conversation from earlier? This is an example of using an impact question. "How do you think the extra expense for the ocean view will affect our overall budget for the trip?" Once others realize how the rest of the trip might suffer just to have an ocean view, they might change their mind or increase the budget. The point is to make sure everyone understands the various impacts in the context of the actual conversational topic.

Reverse Questions

How many of you have friends and family who ask you questions? Of course, we all do. Have you ever had friends or family members ask you a question and you had no clue what they were asking? What did you do? You ask a reverse question like, "What are you talking about?" They answered you by giving you more information and clarifying what they asked. The purpose of a reverse question is to get to the real question so you can answer it at the right time.

Here are two rules from the selling world that apply*:

- The question someone asks is never the real question.
- The intention of the question is always more important than the content of the question.

If you believe either of these rules to be true, then a reverse question is the answer. When you ask reverse questions, be careful not to sound accusatory, like a police interrogation or an IRS audit. A good reverse question must be conversational, appropriate to the situation, and on topic.

I have been amazed over the years as I teach this concept

---

*   Source: David Sandler.

to observe people who think this means that you are never allowed to answer a question. The purpose of a reverse question is to uncover the real question and answer it at the appropriate time—now or later. One student came to class bragging how he had reversed someone 27 times! Good outcomes will never occur if you think it is a game to see who can ask the most reverse questions.

Let's get back to how you could use a reverse question to uncover the intention of a question you are asked. Let's say I were to ask my wife, "How soon before dinner is ready?" How many possible intentions could there be for that question? (By the way, my wife does not allow me in the kitchen and tells me she enjoys cooking, so she expects that I have no idea what's going on and she would be OK with this question.) Maybe there is something I want to do before or after dinner, and I want to make sure I have time. I could be hungry and want to eat as soon as possible. Perhaps, I want to take her out to dinner—to the restaurant of her choice, of course. Any one of these is a perfectly valid intention for the question.

If my wife believes I am hungry and want to eat as soon as possible but she has not started anything, she might respond, "In just a few minutes," as she frantically prepares something. My guess is her tonality might suggest a mild annoyance.

Perhaps my real question is, "Do you want to go out for dinner tonight?" If I get home and ask her if she wants to go out just as the green beans are hitting the table, there is a good chance she would respond with, "Why didn't you call? I wouldn't have spent the last hour over the stove!" You can imagine the tonality of that message!

To uncover the real intention of my question, she needs to ask a reverse question, or two, and maybe even three.

Me: "How soon before dinner is ready?"

Her: "Why do you ask?"

Me: "Just curious."

Her: "Are you curious for a particular reason?"

Me: "Not really."

Her: "I know you. What are you thinking?"

Me: "I was hoping we could go out tonight, if you haven't started dinner yet."

Her: "Let's go!"

In the above example, I have deflected answering her reverse questions until I know it is safe to ask the real question. I give her intellectual smoke screens until I am far enough into the house and back by the kitchen to see nothing is started. Now I know it is safe to share the intention of my original question. Can you think of a time when you may have done this? It is not uncommon.

There will be times when one simple reverse question is all you need to get to the intention, and thus, the real question.

Me: "What time do we need to leave for the party?"

Her: "You're asking because...?"

Me: "Just checking to see if I have time for a quick shower."

Her: "You should be OK. We have 45 minutes before we need to hit the road."

This example results in a very pleasant Adult-to-Adult conversation. Notice how her response would have been different if we needed to leave in the next 15 minutes. It would have guided my decision appropriately.

> # Alert!
>
> ---
>
> Only use reverse questions to gather more information and understanding. Do not use reverse questions to avoid answering the question; use them to answer the right question.

Multiple-Choice Questions

When you give people choices, it helps them to feel more OK; they feel as if they have some control. This also allows you to become a little not-OK on purpose, to put them at ease. Here is how it works if they are giving you information or asking questions.

When someone shares information about a situation or problem, you can ask a multiple-choice question to gain further clarification and understanding. The multiple-choice question must connect to the situation or problem and include two to four options. More than four options will confuse the other person.

Friends of yours tell you they have a problem with their son who is a freshman at college. His grades are terrible, and his behavior is way out of bounds. A multiple-choice Nurturing Parent question could sound like this: "Sorry to hear you have to deal with this. Do you think it is because this is his first time away from parental supervision? Or has he fallen in with the wrong crowd, or maybe he is just having trouble with the school work and is acting out in frustration? Which do you think it might be?"

In this example, you nurtured by indicating your concern, then you gave several options as to why the problem may be occurring. Now the conversation will flow forward by your friends sharing with you which of those they believe to be the culprit. If it is not one of those, they will share what they think has happened. Either way you gather more information, which will allow you to focus your responses and questions.

When you use a multiple-choice question as a response to a question you have been asked, you are also asking a reverse question. When I asked my wife, "How soon before dinner is ready?," she could have used a multiple-choice reverse question: "Are you asking because you are hungry, because there is something you want to do before or after dinner, or because you want to take me out to dinner?" This would have allowed her to get to the real intention of my question quickly. The key point: More information is gained when you ask a multiple-choice question.

Assumptive Questions

I like to give people the benefit of the doubt. I believe most people to be reasonable and intelligent. Because of this belief, I make assumptions about what they have done. (By the way, to "assume" is not always making an "A.S.S. of U. and M.E.")

When I assume those I'm speaking with did what most people would have done, I ask them how it worked out. An assumptive question after they say, "My drain is clogged," can sound like this: "When you called the plumber to find out how much it would cost to fix, what did he say?" The assumption they called the plumber makes sense. If they haven't called, you can find out why not. If they have called, you will gain more information. More information often leads to better outcomes.

A version of an assumptive question is the presumptive question. It is similar in the fact I presume something was done or is going to be done, and I ask about the outcome. You might say to your teen who is asking permission to stay out all night, "So, when I call your friend's parents to make sure they are OK with this sleepover, what do you think they will say?" The presumption that I will call the other kid's parents should elicit more information.

Another version is, "So when I called your friend's parents, what do you think they said?"—which might elicit an even more interesting response! There is a subtle difference between presuming you will do it and presuming you have already done it.

Pain Questions

One of the often misunderstood tools I use frequently is the Sandler Pain Funnel®. Many folks take the funnel literally and believe it is a series of exactly worded questions to ask whenever someone brings you a problem. My take on the Pain Funnel is different. I believe it helps you to know the answers you are looking/listening for.

A brilliant coworker once told me, "Knowing what you are looking for helps you recognize it when you see it." This wisdom applies to the Pain Funnel. Also, knowing what you are listening for helps you recognize it when you hear it. The Pain Funnel is a series of the types of questions I have been sharing with you.

When people bring their problems to you, start by asking, "What's going on?" There are hundreds of ways to ask them to tell you more about the problem. Choose a **"tell me more"** question that is situationally appropriate and comfortable coming out of your lips.

PAIN QUESTIONS

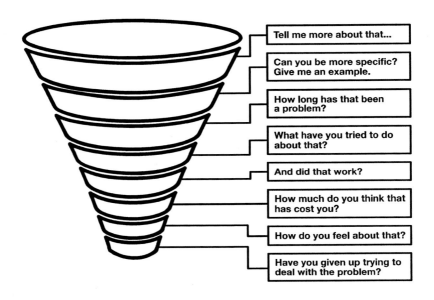

Tell me more about that...
Can you be more specific? Give me an example.
How long has that been a problem?
What have you tried to do about that?
And did that work?
How much do you think that has cost you?
How do you feel about that?
Have you given up trying to deal with the problem?

If they don't get into details, don't be afraid to ask, "Could you be **more specific** or perhaps share an example with me?" These scope-and-significance questions will give insight into what is happening.

The next thing to ask is **how long** the situation or problem has been going on. If it has recently occurred, the breadth and depth may not yet be apparent. If it has been going on for many months or even years, find out why it has now become important.

When you further **uncover the details**, you uncover

the real reasons and then, by default, the real problem. Remember the rule that states the problem they bring you is never the real problem. Uncover the answers to these initial funnel questions and you will have a better understanding of the real problem.

Knowing what they have already tried to do to fix the problem is critical. If people are confiding in you, the last thing you want to give them is the same advice as the previous three people they asked. Be a listener and ask, "What have you done to try to fix it?" I like to use a nice assumptive question here—a version of, "When you did what you should have done to fix it, what happened?" You will want to soften the phrasing and make sure it is situationally appropriate. Listen carefully to the answer; it will tell you the proper direction to take the conversation.

Alert!

When you ask an assumptive question, you must be careful of your tonality. You don't want to sound condescending or like a smart-aleck.

Acknowledgment Questions

When you need to be sure others accept the truth or existence of the facts being discussed or of the problem or issue you or they want to discuss, an acknowledgment question is appropriate to ask.

An acknowledgment question comes directly from your active listening. Listen to what the other person is telling you; then ask the appropriate question so the answer acknowledges you are both discussing the same topic or issue.

- ◆ "Here are the issues we have uncovered: Issue 1, Issue 2, and Issue 3. Are we on the same page?"
- ◆ "If I heard you correctly, what you are asking me to do is to suspend your 11 P.M. curfew for this one special event. Am I correct?"
- ◆ "So, if I am hearing the board correctly, shareholders are expecting significant dividends for the next quarter, and if they don't get them, they will be expecting significant changes in management. Is that right?"

The other person's answer should acknowledge the fact you are both understanding the facts or requests. The other person is stating an understanding of the actual problem or issue being discussed.

Confirmation Questions

Confirm what you think you heard the other person say by asking a confirmation question. This is used frequently when you actively listen to the other person and typically is less formal than the acknowledgment question. Remember when we discussed no mutual mystification? Confirmation questions help to keep things clear. You are confirming what you think you heard.

- "Did you just ask for a raise in your allowance?"
- "Are you telling me the show tickets are for tomorrow night?"
- "When you say as soon as possible, what are you really hoping for?"
- "There will be no executive bonuses this year, correct?"

I recall when I was discussing a performance review with my administrative assistant, and I asked her, "So, how are you doing at meeting all of the deadlines?" She looked at me puzzled and asked this confirmation question, "Why would I be beating dead lions?" What I thought I said and what she heard were entirely different. Thankfully, she asked for clarification. Notice it wasn't a formal, "Did I just hear you ask me about beating dead lions?" But it was an attempt to confirm what she thought she heard me say.

With a confirmation question, you want to clarify a word, an intention, or a definition. If it sounds unclear, ask. Remember, no mutual mystification.

The Importance of Questions

Questions help you gather information and are tools to use when actively listening. The more information you gather, the better judgments you can make as to which decision would be most appropriate. This would include decisions like which question to ask next, what action would be most helpful on your part, or perhaps whether or not to end the conversation until you can gather the appropriate information to further positive progress on the conversation's topic. When deciding important issues with coworkers, family members, or friends, gathering more information from them first through the appropriate use of questions will always allow you to make better decisions and achieve more positive outcomes.

CHAPTER 5

Listen and Talk

Listening: The Art of Paying Attention

L et me state the obvious. To listen to other people, you must pay attention to them—which means listening with your eyes as well as your ears. With all the distractions of the modern world—smart phones, computers, and the like—paying attention to what another person is saying has become problematic. Communication on devices such as these does not allow for listening. To truly listen, stop texting, emailing, or posting and instead have a face-to-face conversation.

Meaningful conversations about important topics have better outcomes when they occur face to face. Why? Because, as I've said, 93% of the meaning of a conversation is in physiology and tonality. If all you use are the words, most of the meaning is missed. So, as this chapter progresses, it is with a face-to-face mindset.

Let me share some information which differentiates how people listen.[*]

> There are four styles of listeners, and depending on which style you employ, you may be helping communication or stopping it completely.
>
> "Competitive listeners" may be making eye contact, they may appear to be listening, but they are actually waiting for a break in the conversation to jump in with their own thoughts and ideas. After all, they're much smarter than you.
>
> "Combative listeners" are similar to competitive, but they don't wait for a break in the conversation. They appear to not be really listening at

---

[*]   Source: Sandler Training.

all—they may interrupt, talk over you, and, worst of all, not even realize they're doing it.

"Passive listeners" may really be listening, but they give no indication. They don't acknowledge points; they don't ask questions. Their eyes and minds may be wandering away from the conversation.

Finally, "active listeners" are involved with small interjections of acknowledgments and validations. They ask clarifying questions, they paraphrase the speaker's words back to them to ensure understanding. They're listening with their whole being and are completely involved in the conversation.

After [reading] the four descriptions, it's rather obvious which type of listener is the most effective. The question is, what kind of listener are you? If you're not actively listening in every exchange, how can you improve?

The art of paying attention requires effort, and therefore energy, on your part. To be an active listener requires the ability to put your ego on the shelf and to give up your need to be right, which we mentioned earlier. It also requires you to not just wait for your turn to talk, as suggested earlier as well. To be a true artist in the art of paying attention, you must have a sincere desire to truly understand the other person so all can reach a positive outcome.

Active Listening

People talk a lot about active listening and how important it is to understanding other people. Why? Because it is! Any communication class will teach you how important it is to clarify and make sure the intended message sent is the actual message received. This is a two-way responsibility on both the sender (talker) and receiver (listener), and active listening is a skill both people need to possess to communicate more effectively for more positive outcomes. In previous chapters, we have talked about certain types of questions and how people can misunderstand the message. To make sure the other person understands what you mean, ask questions as part of active listening.

Anything other than total concentration and focus on the current conversation you are engaged in can lead to misunderstanding and outcomes that are not optimal. If you are not focused, concentrating, or paying attention, you cannot actively listen because you are not actively engaged in the conversation.

Active Listening Techniques

There are two ways to reflect
the speaker's message:

Restatement

Paraphrasing

Many people do not realize active listening requires them to talk. When you talk during active listening, it is usually to ask a question. I recall a time many years ago when I was not totally engaged in the conversation. The other person said to me, "You're bean sweet." I had never heard the term "bean sweet" before, but I didn't question it at the time. Weeks later I had the occasion to interact with the same person, so I asked her what "bean sweet" meant. She was confused, since she didn't recall ever having said it. Once I reminded her of the context and conversation, she began to laugh and said, "No, what I said is, you were being sweet!" Oops, my bad!

Since I am sharing how bad I have been throughout my life with active listening, let me share another memory. I was at a neighborhood party one summer afternoon when a couple arrived that I knew very well. She was about eight months pregnant. When I greeted them, I enthusiastically and in fun, said to her, "Hi, preggie!" Had I been listening with my eyes I would have noticed her upset look as she hurried away from me. As the party continued, I did notice she was avoiding me. As I was leaving I went over to her to say goodbye—and if looks could kill, I was finished. Finally, I asked what was wrong. She informed she was upset with me because I had called her "piggy" upon her arrival. My horrified reaction and apology saved the day that time.

Hopefully, people learn from their mistakes. I know I received the lesson loud and clear back then. Now when I notice my words or actions eliciting an unexpected response, I stop and ask, "I get the feeling there is an issue with what I just said. Are you feeling the same?" Close the feedback loop with active listening and make sure the message you intended to send is the message the other person heard.

Restatement

Active listening is nothing more than making sure you heard what you thought you heard. Many times, this can be confirmed by simply parroting back to the person what you thought you just heard. To parrot means you repeat what you heard and ask if that is what was meant.

An example: "Take out the garbage and clean my room before going out, right?" (All parents hope their teenager understands them as clearly!)

Paraphrasing

When you listen to other people and they share factual information such as, dates, times, locations, or personal feelings, often confirming is a statement rather than a question. It can be as simple as saying: "I understand. You are upset because you thought we were meeting at 3 P.M."

> ## Alert!
> _____
> Oddly enough, to listen effectively you need to truly do some talking. You talk when you ask clarifying or confirming questions.

No Wishy-Washy Words

"Good chance" is a phrase I have heard many times in my life. What does good chance really mean?

A client informed me, "There's a good chance I'll be there."

I said, "90/10 you're there, 90/10 you're not, or 50/50?"

He said, "50/50."

I responded, "So, you're not coming."

And he replied, "No."

Whenever you hear a wishy-washy word or something less than clear, ask what the other person truly means. There is no reason to act on or believe the wishy-washy words will ever come to pass. Clear it up. Use one of the questioning strategies that I have shared. Good questions are a form of active listening.

Who remembers the movie *Dumb and Dumber*? Do you recall the line, "So you're telling me there's a chance?" Jim Carrey's character Lloyd heard what he wanted to hear from Mary, played by Lauren Holly. He ignored her physiology, which was communicating quite the opposite. Be careful. This is not active listening. This is a case of "happy ears." "Happy ears" occur when you only hear what you want to hear and ignore the verbal or nonverbal messages to the contrary.

Silence

Believe it or not, silence can be a cue to the other person of your undivided attention. Obviously, I am not talking about your silence because you were distracted and not listening to them. In an article for *World of Psychology*, here is what Kurt Smith, Psy.D., LMFT, LPCC, AFC, says about silence.

In reality, silence can be a very effective communication tool. Communication is simply about conveying a message, and sometimes silence can do that better than any words.

You may have heard the statistic that 93% of communication is nonverbal. It comes from research by Dr. Albert Mehrabian. He found that words convey only 7% of our message, while the rest of communication occurs through our tone, volume, facial expressions, gestures, posture, and the like. So if the majority of communication is nonverbal, doesn't it make sense that silence could be good communication?

In relationships, communication often becomes a game of one-upmanship, rather than an exchange of ideas. The goal becomes to get the last word or have your idea win out, instead of a sharing of ideas. When communication functions in this way in a relationship, division is fostered rather than unity. It's no wonder that "communication problems" is the top problem cited by partners coming to couples counseling.

Smith goes on to offer three compelling reasons that using silence in your communication is worth considering:

- **Silence helps you clarify and refine your message instead of blathering on.** Let's face it: Smith is right about this. Talking too much is a common problem, one that few people can claim never to have encountered. It's far too easy to fall into the trap of talking a subject to death, with the result that others miss the point. The discipline of silence forces you to use fewer words to get the message across and helps to deliver a stronger, more direct message.

- **Silence helps you process what the other person is saying.** To put it bluntly: Shutting up makes it far more likely you will actually listen to what your conversational partner has to say. Only when you're not talking can you truly focus in on what someone else is saying and at the same time pick up on their nonverbal cues via facial expression, body language, and vocal tonality.

- **Silence helps you get to better, faster resolutions.** Why are you communicating in the first place? Ideally, it's to share information and reach a decision that makes sense to both sides. All too often, talking is about winning or proving that you're right. Silence can remove that static and help reach a point where both parties feel comfortable with the outcome.

Of course, silence can be used in a way that sabotages effective communication, and you have to be careful about that, too. For instance, you may be tempted to use silence to punish or hurt someone or to show how angry you are with someone's behavior. This is a common feature of abusive relationships, and it's important to notice and avoid that cycle. It's just as important, though, to understand that silence can be a powerful positive force in your communication, even if you've had bad experiences with it in the past.

Thoughtful silence could be your best choice because it gives you time to think before responding. I use the word SILENCE as an acronym to help remember the ways silence can become an effective communication choice.

- **Situation:** Think about the situation. Recall the big picture and do your best not to get emotionally hooked on a particular detail or word of the moment. Take the time, in silence, to process the people, place, and purpose of the conversation.
- **Intensity:** Think about the intensity of emotions currently manifesting. Are you or the other person

caught up in your Child ego state and allowing emotions to control the direction and content of the conversation? Silence could allow the initial intense emotions to subside enough to continue in a meaningful conversation.

- **Listen:** Think about what the other person is saying. When they talk, be silent, look interested, and make eye contact. One of the many mistakes I have made when communicating is jumping in to start talking before others have finished what they were saying. Most times my behavior has set the conversation back. Had I just remained silent and listened to them, when I did start to speak it would have been more focused and related to what they really said.

- **Empathy:** Think about what the other people are dealing with. Put yourself in their shoes, and, in the silence, imagine how you would be communicating if the roles were reversed. When you do your best to get the complete picture from all perspectives, communication results will tend to be more positive.

- **Nurture:** Think about whether you have been communicating from your Nurturing Parent ego state. Empathy and nurturing go hand in hand. Ask yourself how you can best be nurturing in your response to keep the conversation moving in a positive direction. Remember, if you are demanding, directing, or belittling, you are not nurturing.

- **Choices:** Think about your choices. Use the silence to determine which choice would be best. Ask yourself, "Have I been using my communication skills in the most effective way possible? Do I need to do something differently?" You are constantly making choices. Are the choices coming from your fast, knee-jerk-reaction brain or from your slow, thoughtful brain? When you think in the silence, there is a better chance for your thoughtful brain to come up with more and better choices.

- **Exhale:** Think about breathing. When engaged in fast-paced, emotionally charged conversations, people sometimes forget to breathe. Use the silence to take in a few deep breaths and exhale fully. This allows freshly oxygenated blood to get to your brain so it thinks faster, better, and appropriately.

I concur with Dr. Kurt Smith. We are not talking about using silence as a weapon or a means to punish someone. Use silence to further understanding and to think before you respond. A silent pause before answering a question lets the other person know you are giving thought to what has been said.

Talking: The Art of Self-Awareness

You must be self-aware of what you want to communicate and of the physiology, tonality, and words used to deliver your message.

The art of self-awareness is crucial to achieving more positive outcomes in your conversations. Words have power in two ways. First, the actual words you choose are important. Secondly, the physiology and tonality with which you deliver your words can drastically alter the meaning of what you say. Awareness of this will help you communicate what you truly want to communicate. It is a constant battle to ensure you select your words to convey your message and to deliver those words in a manner congruent with your intentions. Have you ever heard yourself saying, "That's not what I meant to say," or "No, I didn't mean it that way"?

I believe carelessness causes communication catastrophes. It sure has in my experience. Carelessness can mean you are not truly listening or you have not given your response enough thought. It can also mean you haven't chosen your words wisely, which leaves you vulnerable to misunderstandings.

Alert!

Carelessness causes communication catastrophes!

When people suffer from lazy listening, they become careless in the words they choose in response. You need to have a high level of self-awareness as you communicate to avoid lazy listening, which results in careless words. Wouldn't it be great to never again have to say: "I am sorry—that is not what I meant"?

To make sure your talking is most effective, it requires you to listen with your eyes by observing the physiology of others as they respond to your words. As you see how they respond, you will be able to adjust your physiology and tonality or rephrase what you just said. To accomplish this, self-awareness is critical. Being aware of how your words, tone, and physiology affect people is a skill to be mastered.

Words Are Labels

The words you choose are nothing more than mental names for your mind's representations of the things and actions in the world around you. You can communicate with others because you and they have agreed to the same names for the same things or actions. Words are labels.

When there is a conflict in the definition of the words being used, conflict and misunderstanding can arise. The labels (words) you place on people and things can have a negative impact. Research out of the Ohio State University from Darcy Haag Granello and Todd Gibbs makes this point rather dramatically.

Granello's and Gibbs's research found participants in the study showed less tolerance toward people who were labeled as "the mentally ill" versus people who were labeled as "people with mental illnesses."

Granello said in an article in *Science Daily*, "The language we use has real effects on our levels of tolerance for people with mental illness." In the same article, Gibbs said, "Person-first language is a way to honor the personhood of an individual by separating their identity from any disability or diagnosis he or she might have." He went on to say, "When you say 'people with a mental illness,' you are emphasizing that they aren't defined solely by their disability. But when you talk about 'the mentally ill,' the disability is the entire definition of the person."*

Can these findings have a similar impact in your conversations with family and friends? I believe so. Words have a way of reflecting beliefs and biases. The words you use and how you hear the other person's words all travel through the filter of each person's belief system.

One of the reasons President Ronald Reagan was dubbed the "Great Communicator" was his word choices. It has been said he spoke at a level that resonated with most of the country. The level is determined by the words he used. Let's relate this to OK/Not-OK theory. If you want to make people feel not-OK, use words they do not understand or maybe have never heard before.

Whenever you use esoteric language, such as words or information only people in the "know" use, make sure you provide your listener or reader with clarification. If you are using big words to sound smarter than others, do a self-awareness check and question your motivation. This could be an example of a lack of communication integrity. At the very least, explain what unfamiliar words

---

* Grabmeier, Jeff, "Why you should never use the term 'the mentally ill,'" Ohio State News, January 26, 2016, news.osu.edu/news/2016/01/26/person-first.

mean. For an example, look back at the first sentence of this paragraph.

Pay Attention

Self-awareness of the words you use and how they affect people is critical. When you pay attention to the words you use while talking, you increase your chances of: one, mutual understanding; two, keeping the people with whom you are communicating OK; and three, increasing the odds of a positive outcome. Again, this will require energy and effort on your part combined with a sincere desire to achieve more positive outcomes as you communicate with others.

CHAPTER 6

The Attitude

Attitude Is Mental

No doubt you have heard how important your attitude is when it comes to doing anything. The phrase "getting your head on straight" comes to mind. The mental part of the endeavor, whether it be sports, arts, or living life, refers to your attitude. I define attitude as what you think and feel in your mind. It is everything going on between your ears.

I believe your attitude is either positive or negative about any behavior or endeavor you undertake in life. To this day, I thank my dad for teaching me to expect positive outcomes. When I first began my sales career, just after college, he gave me some simple advice. He told me to expect a positive outcome at the end of each sales appointment. It didn't have to be a sale, necessarily, but rather everyone feeling better for having had the meeting. This advice has stayed with me throughout my sales career and in life. In this chapter I will explore how your attitude can help you to achieve effective and efficient outcomes in your communications.

Born a "10"

During my work with sales training I learned about Identity/Role Theory. The simple version of I/R Theory is found in this rule: "You can only perform your roles in life in a manner consistent with how you see your-self conceptually."* Your roles in life are the things you do, such as being a parent, a spouse, a golfer, a teacher, or whatever you decide to do. I think you get the point. Roles are much like what you see in a movie. We all know Matt Damon is not Jason Bourne in real life. Jason Bourne is one of the many roles he plays in movies.

---

* Source: Sandler Training.

Separating who you are from what you do is important if you are to have meaningful conversations. Your identity, who you truly are, is not the same as the roles you choose to perform. Your communication with others should take this into account.

How you value your identity, the real you, is vital to success in your various roles. Psychologists have used the 1–10 scale to illustrate the point. People rate their self-worth, or identity, from one to ten. Ten is the highest, and one is the lowest. The people who rate themselves in the 8–10 area are called psychological winners and will tend to outperform people who rate their identity lower. Those who rate themselves 1–3 are referred to as psychological non-winners, and those who rate themselves in the middle, 4–7, are referred to as at-leasters. At-leasters don't win, but at least they don't lose.

Psychological winners tend to be goal setters who take responsibility for their actions. They don't blame things outside of their control. If they planned an outdoor birthday party for their child and it begins to rain 30 minutes prior to the party, they don't blame the weather for ruining the party. They accept the reality and make the appropriate adjustment, like moving the party indoors.

Another interesting thing about psychological winners is

they don't take things personally. If they fail at a role, they learn the lesson, adjust, and make another attempt at role success. Psychological winners fail their way to success. While confident, psychological winners tend to be humble and treat others as having the same self-worth, whether the other person's self-concept believes it or not.

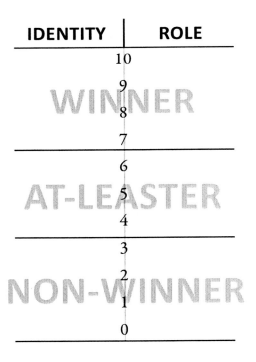

On the other hand, psychological non-winners (people who rate themselves 1–3) will fail and continue to fail because they do not get the lesson. They keep doing the same things that caused the failure. Then they blame someone or something else. Many psychological non-winners can come off as egotistical and treat others in a demeaning manner. This will give the psychological non-winner a false sense of having more value.

When you communicate with others as if you all have an inherent value of 10, you communicate on a level playing field that allows for more positive outcomes.

My hope is for you to pay attention to past communication failures, analyze why they failed, learn the lesson, make any adjustments, and not blame the other person. That's right! Act as if you are an "I"-10!

Alert!

Psychological winners take responsibility. Psychological non-winners make excuses.

How you rate your inherent value as a human being is vital to your success in communicating for more positive outcomes. Let's look at how to arrive at an identity rating.

Childhood Conditioning

Using the 1–10 scale of worthiness from the above example, when each human being is born, their inherent worth is a 10. This means all people are born with a worth of 10 just because they are human beings. Throughout life right up to the moment of death, people remain human beings. So, that value of 10 as a human being never diminishes. Then why do some value themselves lower than a 10 throughout their lives? It's because of the childhood conditioning that equated role success with value as a human being.

What messages did you internalize as a child? The answer to this question dictates much of your adult choices. The instant you were born, you were bombarded with messages from others as to who you are and what you should do. Most of these messages came from parents and other family members who interacted with you in childhood. I believe most people like this truly mean well (although, I am not naïve enough to believe that is always the case).

People are conditioned from birth. They learn the rules of life and the consequences of not following the rules. They also learn what others believe their inherent worth to be. If they get the message of being more worthy by following the rules and doing what is expected in their role performances, such as student, child, playmate, etc., then their self-worth gets tied to their role performance.

- "Why can't you get good grades like your sister?"
- "Why can't you be a good boy like your brother?"
- "Good little boys and girls get a Christmas gift, and bad little boys and girls get a lump of coal."
- "You're a bad child. Good children don't do that!"
- "What's wrong with you? Can't you do any-thing right?"

The above messages subconsciously devalue a child's self-worth by tying it directly to role performance. It is a way of saying, "You only have value if you do what I think you should do. And only if you do it well."

There is a better way to communicate with children. Separate who they are from what they do. A message like this can make a huge difference. It could sound like this: "You are my child and I love you, but what you are doing is not acceptable."

If you start with something like the above, it is much easier to move into a conversation about what the expected behavior is and what the consequences of continuing the behavior will be. Notice how you can manage expectations, get mutual agreement, and be clear on outcomes. You can do all of this without demeaning the child's value as a human being.

Beliefs

Beliefs are the filters through which you experience your version of reality. My mother pointed at a red object and said, "Red." My belief of what constituted the color red began in that moment. Later, my belief about the color red became altered as I learned the nuances of red. I could see the difference between the colors of scarlet, crimson, and rose red. I learned how to generalize my belief and allow new information to alter my belief about the color red.

If I believed the color was scarlet, crimson, or red and I expected people to be specific in talking about colors, the following dialogue might occur. Someone says to me, "Look at the red ball." My response could be, "No, it's a scarlet ball." We could end up arguing about the true color of the ball based on the nuances of the filters (beliefs) we each held regarding the preciseness of color. There is no resolution to this type of disagreement due to the fact we are both correct according to our beliefs. Notice how our specific behavioral style might cause such a disagreement. If I am a High-Compliant, I would need to be right!

Many things that I believed to be true as I grew up were simply the things my grandparents and parents believed to be true. I am reminded of a conversation with a friend in my college years. Her parents kept telling her she was not the "athletic" type. We were talking about getting into a co-ed volleyball league, and she was declining to participate because she was not athletic. Her parents' belief had become hers. She missed out on some great fun.

Beliefs effect communication in many ways. If someone says something that contradicts your belief about a certain topic, you might tend to experience selective hearing. Selective hearing occurs when your mind immediately dismisses the contradicting information as if you didn't even hear what was said. Or, you might immediately get hooked emotionally, causing you to hear only the challenge to your belief; then you might do all you can to justify and defend your belief. When this happens, you are not open and receptive to the valid information that might shift your perception and allow for a change in what you believe to be true.

I recall a time when one of my sons and I were debating about the leading presidential candidates. He was adamantly declaring how unfit my candidate of choice was for the office, and the conversation was a bit heated but certainly not out-of-control. I remember urging him to look at facts and not only the spin. He urged me to do the same.

After the conversation, I began to receive emails from him referring me to various essays and articles. I read the material he had forwarded to me, and guess whose belief shifted? Mine! Because I took the time to look at my belief from a different perspective and to hear the various sides of the argument, I overcame the tendency of selective hearing and made a change in what I filtered out based on my old belief.

Comfort Zones

Habits are hard to break. One of the jobs of your brain/ mind is to keep you feeling normal. Everyone defines normal differently. Often, normal is based on how you see yourself conceptually. If you are a psychological winner (8–10), normal is succeeding in most of your roles in life and, when not succeeding, getting the lesson and taking responsibility. If you are a psychological non-winner, normal is not succeeding and, when you do, possibly self-sabotaging so that weird success doesn't happen again.

After doing the same behaviors over and over, those behaviors become people's comfort zone. This becomes entrenched in how those people value themselves. It becomes what they define as normal.

Whenever you allow your self-worth, childhood conditioning, beliefs, and comfort zones to become rigid and inflexible, you limit your ability to communicate for more positive outcomes.

Alert!

You can only perform about one above or one below how you see yourself conceptually. This is your comfort zone.

You Get What You Expect

I have always liked the quote sometimes attributed to Abraham Lincoln: "Most folks are about as happy as they make their minds up to be." Another of my favorites is from Henry Ford: "If you think you can do a thing or think you can't do a thing, you're right." These two quotes nail the importance of attitude. While it seems simple—you get what you expect—the reality is most of the expectations people fill their minds with are unfocused and negative. This makes it much harder to achieve positive outcomes. Your attitude will drive your goals and behaviors and influence your ability to learn new skills, which would allow you to communicate. Where have your beliefs come from, how are they affecting your attitude (positive or negative), and are you stuck in your comfort zone? Asking yourself these questions and gaining self-awareness of how the answers influence your communication skills will lead you to more successful conversations.

CHAPTER 7

Emotional Involvement

The Emotional Mind

People all have emotions and experience them daily. Whenever you hear yourself say, "I am happy/mad/glad/sad/angry/joyous...," you name the feeling; it is an emotional reaction to what is occurring in your world or in your mind, at a moment in time.

Understanding the connection between your emotions and your mind is critical to more productive outcomes in your communications. All emotions/feelings produce chemical reactions in the human body, including the brain.

In his book, *Thinking, Fast and Slow*, Daniel Kahneman writes that the human brain works at two speeds. This is an important factor in attempting to improve communications with others. Thinking quickly usually happens with little effort and tends to be automatic. Whenever mental effort is applied, it requires people to think slowly.

If you make a quick assessment and respond fast, your communication can suffer. I have been guilty on many occasions of jumping to a quick, knee-jerk reaction after the third word out of the other person's mouth. My response usually comes from my Critical Parent or Rebellious Child ego state. Of course, such a response tends to cause the other person to become not-OK; meaningful communication becomes nearly impossible at this point because emotions create adrenalin, which further shuts down the critical, slower, thinking brain and elicits a fight-or-flight response.

Listening allows your slower thinking brain to concentrate on what is being said and results in better communications. In my case, this would mean to listen to the entire thought the other person is sharing, take time to process my response, and create a more meaningful dialogue.

Keep Your Belly-Button Covered

Have you ever noticed when people say they're feeling things in their gut? Sometimes that is referred to as a "gut reaction." This directly relates to emotions. Since my belly-button is in my gut area, my psychological anchor to keep from getting emotionally involved is to cover my belly-button, literally.

A real test of keeping my belly-button covered occurred recently as I ran an errand. As I drove through the parking lot to park and mail a package, I noticed an awkwardly parked car. I slowed and saw that there appeared to be an agitated male driver talking to the female in the passenger's seat. I parked and took care of my business.

As I left the store, the car was no longer where it had been. The same car was now in a remote area, and I could hear a loud, obviously upset male voice. My fast-thinking brain stopped me about 15 yards from the other car, thinking, "This could turn ugly for the woman." I decided I had better watch to see what happens, just in case she needed help. So, I did. By observing, my "slow" thinking brain was getting the time to strategize.

Within moments, the young male driver exited the car, ranting and raving. He went to the passenger side, opened the door, and pulled the young woman out of the car, all the while yelling at her in a rage. My fast-thinking brain wanted to go confront the man for assaulting the woman. But my slow thinking brain took over, and I began to strategize what to do. With the thought of potential violence, I could feel the adrenalin rush through my body. I was now emotionally involved and thinking how I should respond, but my fast-thinking brain, fueled with adrenalin, only suggested two choices: fight or flight. But, I continued to observe, all the while doing my best to keep my emotions in check. I actually physically covered my belly-button with my left hand.

Sure enough, the young man saw me watching and turns towards me and says, "What the [expletive deleted] are you looking at?" I did not respond. I thought to myself, "Keep your belly-button covered. Do not respond emotionally." He walked toward me asking the same question more loudly and with more anger in his face. I still did not respond.

When he is about 10 feet away he shouted, "I asked you what the [expletive deleted] are you looking at?"

My response, "You."

He glares and says, "Why the [expletive deleted] are you looking at me?"

I say, "Because you remind me of when I was young."

He wasn't expecting that response and looked puzzled. (Thank heaven my slow-thinking brain came up with a strategy.)

I continued, "When I was about your age, I was in a relationship with a woman. We argued one afternoon, and I became so upset and out of control that I nearly did something to land me in jail. After I cooled down, I realized I was giving over control when I lost my temper. I vowed to never allow it to happen again." I was on a roll. "I can't believe you feel good about yourself when you're this out of control, do you?"

He quickly replied with, "No, I don't but she—"

I cut him off. "It doesn't matter what she said. You allowed her to push your buttons and influence the type of person you became. You need to take a deep breath and ask yourself why you allowed it to happen. It has nothing to do with her and everything to do with who you want to be."

Calming down, he said, "I never thought of it that way before, but you're right."

We shook hands, and he walked back to his car much calmer and in control of his emotions. He apologized to the woman.

The point I want to make with this story: You must cover your belly-button if you are to de-escalate increasingly unproductive emotional responses in your conversations. I had to make the conscious choice to not respond emotionally as I watched this whole scene play out and became a participant. Take the time to allow your slow-thinking brain to come up with additional choices, other than just the emotional ones.

It's Your Choice

Think back to a time when you were engaged in a conversation with your spouse, child, coworker, or friend and the emotions you were feeling kept the conversation from being productive. Most people do not have to think that far into the past to relive such a scenario. My guess is the outcome of your scenario did not end well.

It is easy to see how emotional reactions can influence a person's attitude toward a positive or negative response. While you may be unable to choose how you react emotionally, you can always choose how you respond. As I said earlier, I urge you to respond from the Nurturing Parent and Adult ego states.

If emotions and your Child ego state seem to be taking over, it often elicits the fight-or-flight response. If you must, rather than fight and have an unproductive conversation in which you say things you may regret, choose flight. Come back to the topic later when both parties are better able to converse as Adults and Nurturing Parents.

Something else that could help is to report your feelings to the other person before you respond. It could sound like this: "Based on the conversation so far, I am feeling quite upset. Why do you think I'm feeling this way?" Notice how you're asking an awareness question. When others become aware of how they are affecting the people with whom they are communicating, there is a chance for them to adjust and pursue a more productive strategy.

All people have emotional reactions to nearly everything happening to them and around them. I suggest you do your best to slow your thinking and respond in a more productive way. Whenever I allow my fast-thinking brain to react emotionally, the conversation does not end well.

Alert!

Choosing how you respond to your emotional reactions is your choice.

Choose the Right Brain

It is natural to have an emotional reaction to everything that happens to you. But there is a difference from reacting emotionally and responding appropriately. It is the fast-thinking brain that tends to go with the emotional reaction and the slow-thinking brain that comes up with a more appropriate response. Once again, self-awareness has a role to play in keeping unproductive emotional reactions in check. Become aware of which part of your brain is wanting to respond and make the conscious choice to respond appropriately rather than simply react emotionally. This plays into the different ego states discussed earlier. When you stay in your Nurturing Parent and Adult ego states, you will achieve more positive outcomes.

CHAPTER 8

The Outcomes

Managing Outcomes

Outcomes always happen. Every time you engage in a persuasive conversation with another human being, there is an outcome. Outcomes are either positive or negative; there is no neutral. You either get what you want or you don't. Other people either understand your point of view or they don't. A decision to table the conversation to a later date is a positive outcome as is a decision to agree to disagree. Positive outcomes occur when both parties agree about what is to happen next. The conversation on the topic is over or mutually-agreed-upon to continue later. All the skills and concepts previously discussed should lead you to more positive outcomes.

Negative outcomes happen when agreement does not occur and the topic is left open with no clear future or no closure. Generally, both parties feel upset and frustrated with each other. This usually means neither one gets what they want and both are feeling dissatisfied.

The best way to manage outcomes is to deal with them by using mutual agreements at the beginning of the conversation. It is not uncommon for people to engage in a conversation with different expectations about the outcome. I might hope for a resolution to what I perceive as the problem, while my wife may hope to feel listened to and understood at the end of the conversation. Many books have been written on gender differences and how each listens, processes information, and communicates. At this point, I suggest you be aware that differences always exist between one person and another, and that early on in your conversations, you clarify the expected outcomes. An example could sound like this:

Me: "Sure, I'd be happy to talk about your concerns. Are you expecting me to give you suggestions or to listen so you can talk it through?"

My wife: "Let me talk it through so I can figure out what is really going on."

Me: "Great. So, tell me what's happening."

If this occurs at the beginning of a conversation, you will have a better chance to achieve a positive outcome, especially if the other skills and tactics are used throughout the interaction.

Outcomes Are a Choice

People involved in a conversation always have a choice where outcomes are concerned. If any one of the participants is not seeking a positive outcome, the ensuing conversation becomes fruitless. The question to ask yourself is, "Am I engaging in this conversation to solve a problem; get an answer; understand the other; help the other understand me; ask for help; acquire something; or make a decision?"

If the answer to all of those is "no," the odds of engaging in a productive conversation diminish. It could become simple chit-chat, or it could mean someone is spoiling for a fight. You can control the reason you are engaging in the conversation, which means you take on the responsibility to achieve a positive outcome. You cannot make the same choice for the other person. But, you can find out the reason or purpose for the conversation. The other person may just have the need to unload and may not be seeking a next step or closure.

If you determine from the other person's reasons that there is no clear outcome possible, you can choose to listen or not. I must say, some of my best conversations have occurred when I chose not to respond or drive the conversation to a resolution and instead just listened. Even though the others did not want or expect an "outcome" from the conversation, it became positive because they felt I listened to them. Remember, people want and need to feel they have been heard.

To achieve positive outcomes, define what positive means to you. Take the time to think through the impending conversation and what you are attempting to accomplish. This serves two purposes. First, it gives you time to think and allow the slow part of your brain to gain a clearer perspective and develop a strategy. Second, you will better articulate your desired outcome.

Usually, it is the spur-of-the-moment conversations that cause people to get emotionally involved and lead to angry exchanges. Take the time to plan the important conversations or to postpone the impromptu conversations in which you are not prepared to participate so you can achieve more positive outcomes.

Alert!

Outcomes happen.
It is up to you to control them.

When you can articulate your desired outcome, you now have a goal. Goal accomplishment requires you to do something. In this case, take time to think; then apply the skills and strategies suggested in this book. It requires your energy, time, and attention. Productive conversations about the important things in your life do not just happen.

Take Control of the Outcomes

It is up to you to communicate for positive outcomes. When you leave the outcome to the other person, you may be sadly disappointed. When you need to have that important conversation, don't leave it to chance. Get agreements up front regarding the time, topic, and hoped-for outcome at the end of the conversation. You must make sure the other participant is willing and able to invest the time and energy to engage in a productive conversation for the purpose of coming to a positive outcome.

CHAPTER 9

Growing Together

Building Relationships

Growing together does not mean you get stuck to each other. It means as each person in a relationship grows, the relationship also grows. Relationships are made up of individuals doing their best to connect, relate, and communicate with each other. Most people have a handful or two of people with whom it is important to them to have a deep, meaningful relationship. I believe communication is the key to rich, productive, and satisfying relationships. This applies to significant others, family members, friends, and coworkers. To explain the concept, I will use significant others as the example.

In the beginning, there was "you" and there was "me." "Us" didn't exist until the two met and developed a relationship. I like to use this analogy: Each was a self-contained circle. The two moved through life expanding or contracting the size of their circles based on their experiences, beliefs, relationships, and ability (or inability) to communicate with each other.

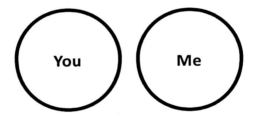

As the two communicate and interact with each other, the circles overlap. They begin to develop a relationship. As the relationship grows and develops, the overlap increases. As people interact with the important others in their lives, they grow by the multiple overlappings with each other.

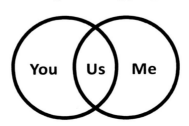

As individual human beings, people should be growing and expanding, which would result in the individual circles growing larger. As people each grow and continue their relationship building, the "us" would also grow and lead to a more meaningful relationship.

If one person grows and the other doesn't, there could be a problem. The person not growing could become totally engulfed by the other person's circle. In this example, too much pressure is put on the relationship and usually leads to a break. Other than when children are very young, if one person relies totally on another person for a sense of self and worth, communication becomes a challenge. The one being engulfed is often so dependent that an effective Adult-to-Adult conversation is difficult.

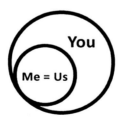

Even if one person grows and the other manages to not become engulfed; they could run the risk of one outgrowing the other. As one grows and the other doesn't, the "us" becomes less of a factor to the one who is growing.

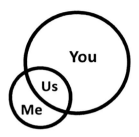

When something like either of the two previous examples happens in a relationship, it is easy to find that the Child or Critical Parent ego states dominate the conversations. One person could feel less important or burdened by the other and could make demands (Critical Parent) or get overly emotional (Child). Basically, the imbalance makes one or the other feel not-OK, and that one may attempt to make the other person more not-OK. This is a recipe for communication disaster.

Communication and time are two key elements in growing a relationship. The more the two communicate effectively with each other, the more the relationship grows. The more time they spend together, the more the relationship grows. The more time they spend together, the greater the chance of engaging in quality communication. The only way to achieve quality time with another is to invest in the quantity of time.

A warning: For both of the two to be growing, they must have experiences outside the immediate relationship with each other and develop as unique individuals. Spending all their time together and only communicating with each other could have a negative impact. It is my belief many relationships stagnate when the circles overlap and become one, creating only an "us."

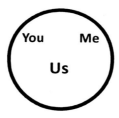

Don't get me wrong. It is very important for each relationship to create a nurturing, growing, expanding "us." Growth comes from experiencing and sharing what each experiences when in the outside world. Without the new things to share, which each brings to the conversation, boredom—or worse—could result.

Interpersonal Goals

To build a relationship with another person, whether it be your spouse, child, sibling, or friend, you must make it a priority. The best way to make it a priority is to make it a goal. Proactively decide which relationships you want to grow, and then do something about it. Any goal, to be meaningful, requires you to take some type of action on a regular, ongoing basis.

In the next several pages I am going to walk you through an interpersonal goal exercise.* You can use it for each person with whom you decide to grow a relationship.

Interpersonal Relationship Developer

Date: _____

I am going to develop my relationship with _____.

1. What are seven positive words that will best describe my relationship with _____ one year before I die?

   ◆ _____

   ◆ _____

   ◆ _____

   ◆ _____

   ◆ _____

   ◆ _____

   ◆ _____

---

*   Source: Adapted from the Sandler Training worksheet of the same title.

2. What is not working in my relationship with

_____? For which elements am I not taking

responsibility? _____

_____

_____

_____

_____

3. What emotions am I holding back from

_____?

Why? _____

_____

_____

_____

_____

4. How can I better show love/care in the way

_____ wants?

_____

_____

_____

_____

_____

5. What are seven lifetime goals I would like to achieve with _____?

   ◆ _____
   ◆ _____
   ◆ _____
   ◆ _____
   ◆ _____
   ◆ _____
   ◆ _____

6. To enrich my relationship with _____ in the next year, I must:

   ◆ _____
   ◆ _____
   ◆ _____
   ◆ _____
   ◆ _____
   ◆ _____
   ◆ _____

7. What are the specific actions I will take?

This Year	Semi-Annual Check-up	Year End Result
I must:		
I will apologize for:		
I will give:		
I will show I care by:		
I will make _____ feel significant by:		
I will stop:		

This Year	Semi-Annual Check-up	Year End Result
I will start:		
I will communicate:		

Develop Relationships

The interpersonal goals exercise gives you a lot to think about when it comes to growing and developing relationships with the people you select, whether it be a spouse, a child, a coworker, or a friend. What do you think the result would be if both of you did the exercise and then discussed it with each other? You guessed it! Communicating with each other about the important things in life will build, grow, and sustain a relationship more quickly than anything else.

CHAPTER 10

Keep Talking

The subtitle of this book, "Communicate with Skill for Positive Outcomes," is more than a slogan. For me, it is my lifelong quest. The sting of being misunderstood is far outweighed by the joys of mutual understanding and respect, which only occur when communication is open, honest, and real.

Both participants must want to achieve more positive outcomes when communicating with each other. If only one of the participants provides the energy better communication requires, the outcome is doomed before it begins. While one person can start the process, true growth in communication between two people is not a one-person endeavor.

To change the outcomes of your communications, work on the behaviors that create more positive outcomes. Manage what you can control. Focus on understanding the other person; listen to understand; talk in a manner that is consistent with how the other person processes information; get mutual agreements (no wishy-washy words); and keep your belly-button covered. With all this in your arsenal, you will achieve more positive results.

There is a reminder posted in my workspace. It reads: "Now that you know better—act like it!" This saying serves as a constant reminder for me to remain vigilant in my quest for better communications. The reality is that knowing better does not always equate to doing better. I urge you to join me in this lifelong journey of self-aware-ness with the destination of improved interpersonal rela-tionships by communicating for more positive outcomes.

Stay ADULT!

ADULT

Acknowledge the opinion of others.

Acknowledging the opinion of others doesn't mean you must agree with them. People all have opinions based on what they believe to be true. Opinions are not right or wrong—they are just opinions. Opinions are formed when information gets filtered through a person's belief system and experiences.

I recall a psychology class in college that described an experiment about how opinions regarding facts can be changed to conform with the majority. Solomon Asch did a conformity study back in the 1950s in which the test subject decided whether to agree with other test subjects, who were all in league with Asch to give an incorrect answer. (I know I said I would not to turn this book into a college textbook, but this experiment is so classic I had to share the highlights. And I did wait until the end.) In a 2008 article for _Simply Psychology_, Saul McLeod summed up the Asch experiment like this:

> Results: Asch measured the number of times each participant conformed to the majority view. On average, about one third (32%) of the participants who were placed in this situation went along and

conformed with the clearly incorrect majority on the critical trials.

Over the 12 critical trials, about 75% of participants conformed at least once and 25% of participants never conformed. In the control group, with no pressure to conform to confederates, less than 1% of participants gave the wrong answer.

Conclusion: Why did the participants conform so readily? When they were interviewed after the experiment, most of them said that they did not really believe their conforming answers but had gone along with the group for fear of being ridiculed or thought "peculiar." A few of them said that they really did believe the group's answers were correct.

Apparently, people conform for two main reasons: because they want to fit in with the group (normative influence) and because they believe the group is better informed than they are (informational influence).*

While there have been more recent experiments indicating the effect may not be as strong as Asch's findings,

---

* McLeod, S. A., "Asch Experiment," SimplyPsychology.org, 2008. Retrieved from www.simplypsychology.org/asch-conformity.html. Date retrieved, September 15, 2017.

there is validity to the reasons people conform and change their opinions. The point I want to make is there are times people conform and create their opinions based on something other than facts. If you are the only voice challenging another's opinion, it is highly unlikely your facts will change their minds. Remember you always have the right to your opinions and the right to respectfully disagree with another's opinion. Very often facts have nothing to do with the differences. Just because you acknowledge another's opinion does not mean you have to agree with it.

<u>D</u>emand nothing in return for your love, friendship, guidance, or assistance.

If you give love, friendship, guidance, or assistance to someone else, give it unconditionally. If others believe that you require something in return for your time or attention, there is a chance your communication with them will suffer. An "I will only do what you want if you do what I want" attitude will not carry you very far toward more positive outcomes. When you choose to communicate your love, friendship, guidance, or assistance in a manner that is open, honest, and free from conditions, you will form a better bond and achieve more positive outcomes.

Don't confuse this with negotiating. If you are going

to give up something during a negotiation, always find out how the other person will reciprocate. You can love your partner without demanding anything in return. However, if my wife and I are negotiating whether we get the thin- or thick-crust pizza, I might agree to the thick crust tonight if we can get thin crust next time. Whenever you agree to reciprocate, be sure you do what you said you would do.

Understand others.

So much of this book has been about understanding others. The more people understand about each other, the easier it is to be tolerant, nonjudgmental, and forgiving. To understand other people, you must communicate with them. The more you understand about them, the better you can communicate with them. Take the responsibility of understanding them before you need to have them understand you so you can adjust your communications to arrive at more positive outcomes. It will then become a never-ending spiral of upward-growing communication and understanding.

Let go of your need to be right.

You have read in the pages in this book how important it is to let go of your need to be right. An intractable need to be right serves no one well when communicating for more positive outcomes. Remember, what you think is right is your belief or opinion. This belief was acquired by you along your journey of life. Just because you are open to a different way of looking at something doesn't mean you must change your belief or opinion. It just means you are open to new information without the need to argue about who is right or wrong.

Time to engage in face-to-face conversations.

Take the time to talk face-to-face with other human beings. In this current age, electronic communications are overwhelming. When communicating by screen, people lose 90% of the meaning—what a price to pay. Looking into people's eyes as you share information or persuade teaches you how to read people and ascertain the true meaning behind the words they choose to use.

Keep Talking!

I have discovered the only way to build a relationship with another person is to communicate with them. When you first meet someone new, the conversation is fresh and uncharted as both parties learn about each other. When the relationship matures and the newness wears off, what keeps the relationship growing?

My simplistic answer is to keep talking. Talk about the mundane things that have happened since the last conversation, and when discussing important topics that require decisions to be made, do your best to use the tools and insights from the previous chapters. You will be communicating with skill and you will achieve more positive outcomes.

APPENDIX

The Art of De-escalation

O ne of the most common communications-related questions I hear is this one: "What's the best way for me to constructively resolve conflict?"

This question is relevant to interactions in the workplace, in the home, and, let's face it, in virtually any other setting where human beings are likely to interact. Its answer is refreshingly simple and easy to implement: "Find a way to de-escalate the exchange as soon as possible, ideally before the situation polarizes, so that the parties can look at all the options open to them with a clear head."

Now, many people don't do this consistently, which is, I think, why conflict is such a common feature of contemporary life. The kind of de-escalation I'm talking about is an art and it does take practice, but it's a life lesson that repays many times over the effort made to learn it.

To understand the best ways to de-escalate as a way of resolving conflict, it helps to look at where conflict comes from in the first place. Conflict arises when the people involved in an exchange get emotionally involved and either fear the consequence of a "loss" or come to feel strongly that they must "win." In other words, conflict happens when the possibility of a win/win outcome where all sides benefit has been ignored or ruled out.

This is an extremely important point to understand. Whenever you decide there is no viable middle ground, that's typically where conflict is going to arise in your life. All too often, when people are in this mindset, they are going to overlook options that could lead to a win/win outcome.

Think of two kids on the playground at recess, arguing with each other. If they both feel like there's no way out, a fistfight ensues. On the other hand, if one or both of the kids decide to look for a way to walk away before the exchange reaches the level of blows being exchanged, the conflict can be avoided. Grownups face the same basic choice.

The problem is, people find it easy to convince themselves that there's no point in even considering ways to de-escalate from a situation that's going south. Why? Often, it's because they feel de-escalating will be perceived as a sign of weakness. This is a mistake. Consider that the most effective leaders are the ones who operate on the "choose your battles" principle—which means understanding and acting on the idea that not every potential battle is worth investing your time, effort, and energy trying to win. Of course, there may well be times when a head-on conflict is appropriate—but you need to choose those times. Indeed, consistently letting someone else determine when it is time go into battle mode is one of the traits of an ineffective leader.

The key here is simply not to get emotionally involved in the conversation. One excellent way to do that is to set a good up-front contract so both sides know in advance what's going to be talked about, and then stick to that agenda.

Even with that precaution, though, difficult situations

can present themselves. Here's the key to dealing with them: The moment you feel yourself getting emotionally involved in a conversation, find a way to step back.

That's the secret to keeping a conflict from escalating. Stepping back doesn't always come easily, but the practice becomes easier when you bear in mind that it's not whether you're right or wrong that matters most, but how good you are at reducing the tension or pressure in the exchange for both yourself and the other person.

Again: Whether you are right or not is not the point. The pertinent question is, what steps can you take to lower the pressure in the exchange?

Lowering the pressure basically means acting like a grownup. It means thinking before you speak. Letting loose and giving the other person a "piece of your mind" is, all too often, synonymous with handing the responsibility for the outcome over to your Child ego state. It means staying away from defining the other person or ascribing motives to them because saying, "Why are you in such a bad mood?" or "I see you're still holding a grudge about such-and-such," will only increase the level of mutual distrust. It means being aware of the other person's situation and experiences because there's a time and place for everything. If the person you're talking to is deeply stressed out about something else, something that's out of your control, this might not be the best time to even have a conversation.

Here's the bottom line: Acting like a grownup means having the courage to walk away when you know that's appropriate. It also means not leaving in such a way as to make sure you get the last word—or so you can be the one who slams the door.

Lower the Temperature

Ideally, you want to walk away with an agreement about when you can continue the conversation. Failing that, you'll want to walk away with the stated intention to pick up the conversation later, at an undetermined time. The point here is to insulate yourself (and the other person) from the heat of the moment.

In the heat of the moment, you are emotionally involved. Once people become emotionally involved in a dispute, the exchange is likely to become about who's right and who's wrong. This is not the best outcome.

Conflict resolution is not about who's right and who's wrong. It's about identifying the best possible outcome, the outcome most likely to benefit both sides. To find that outcome, you will need to move away from the polarized position where both sides are thinking, "My outcome is the best—and yours is terrible."

Here are some "heat of the moment" statements you can use to lower the pressure. Find a few that feel natural to you and try using them the next time you feel yourself tempted to descend into "schoolyard battle" mode.

- "I really think I need a little bit of time to process what you've said. If it's all right with you, I'm just going to take a break and I will re-engage with you tomorrow in the morning so we can work this out."
- "I'm not thinking clearly on this right now. Can we put this off until I've had the time to process it?"
- "I feel that this is escalating. I'm not comfortable with it. Do you mind if we call time out and come back to this later? I think we can accomplish more that way."
- "I think I need to take a break. Can I come back to you later on this afternoon so we can discuss this then?"

Notice that these are all "I" statements. You're focusing on your own feelings, reactions, and opinions, and you're not defining the other person or ascribing any motives to them. You're not even saying what is happening because

people can disagree about that kind of thing. You're saying
how you feel and what you propose doing next.

An alternative using "we" language might be:

* "What do you say we put this on hold until a time
   when we can approach it more constructively?"

What about when it comes time to continue the discussion? In that case, you might opt to use phrases like the
following to lower the "heat of the moment."

* "I get the feeling that you're still upset about this.
   What am I missing?"
* "I'm picking up from your tone of voice that you
   think what I'm suggesting might not work. Am I
   reading that correctly?" [Other person responds.]
   "OK, what am I missing?"
* "When you thought this through, what kind of
   options did you come up with?"
* "As I thought this through, I came up with several
   possible ways to go: A, B, and C, for instance. Are
   any of those worth considering? Or is there some
   other way that I haven't considered yet?"

Notice that all of these questions, if they are to be effective in lowering the conversational temperature, must be

asked in a calm, nurturing way. Notice, too, that each question requires that you listen without judgment to the response you receive.

Disengagement in Action

Sometimes, you can disengage from the emotions of the conflict situation before you even encounter it. Here's a true story that illustrates what I mean. Recently, a friend I'll call Laura complained to me about something that occurred at her church. Laura has volunteered for the past several years to run two different community projects there. Because these projects required space to acquire items, she was provided with a storage closet that she was told would be hers to use for these projects.

A little background is in order here about my friend. She is a self-described neatnik—meaning she likes to take total control of her projects and is extremely organized. Having things in the right place means a lot to her. She invested a lot of time and effort setting up that storage closet.

You can imagine her surprise and distress when she opened the storage closet that was supposed to be "hers" and found that someone had turned all her careful ordering systems into a disaster area. They had thrown all kinds of items into the closet from another project that had nothing to do with her work. She explained, in deep frustration, what a mess the storage closet had become—and then she told me how she was going to confront the pastor for allowing that mess to happen.

I said, "Laura, I'm curious: Why 'confront'? Why do you think that's the right approach?" (In asking this question, I was hoping to help Laura disengage emotionally from the situation and tap into her Adult ego state in assessing the problem.)

She explained that she was upset because she felt her efforts at cleaning up the closet and getting it organized for her projects were being totally disregarded. In other words, she was emotionally involved and taking it personally.

As Laura vented her frustrations, listing all the different ways she was going to set the pastor straight, I had a growing sense that her "confront" strategy was not likely to end with a positive outcome. I asked if she might want to consider taking a different approach.

"What do you mean?" she asked.

"Well, what if you approached the pastor and said, 'I'm confused. I thought the storage closet was for these specific projects. I was wondering how the closet became junked up with these other items.'" (Notice that those are all "I" statements. Delivered in a nurturing way, they can help de-escalate a discussion about a potential conflict area.)

I urged Laura to listen carefully to whatever response the pastor had to this, and then to ask a simple question: "Since I don't work well in disorganization and so we can make sure these projects are successful, what can we do to make sure this won't happen again?"

She actually took my suggestions and reported that the conversation went well, with no one getting upset. Both projects ended up being huge successes. That's a testament to the power of de-escalation!

Look for these other books
on shop.sandler.com:

Prospect the Sandler Way

Transforming Leaders the Sandler Way

Selling Professional Services the Sandler Way

Accountability the Sandler Way

Selling Technology the Sandler Way

LinkedIn the Sandler Way

Bootstrap Selling the Sandler Way

Customer Service the Sandler Way

Selling to Homeowners the Sandler Way

Succeed the Sandler Way

The Contrarian Salesperson

The Sales Coach's Playbook

Lead When You Dance

Change the Sandler Way

Motivational Management the Sandler Way

Call Center Success the Sandler Way

Patient Care the Sandler Way

Winning from Failing

Asking Questions the Sandler Way

Why People Buy

Selling in Manufacturing and Logistics

The Road to Excellence

CONGRATULATIONS!

From the Board Room to the Living Room
includes a complimentary seminar!

Take this opportunity to personally experience the non-traditional sales training and reinforcement coaching that has been recognized internationally for decades.

Companies in the Fortune 1000 as well as thousands of small- to medium-sized businesses choose Sandler for sales, leadership, management, and a wealth of other skill-building programs. Now, it's your turn, and it's free!

You'll learn the latest practical, tactical, feet-in-the-street sales methods directly from your neighborhood Sandler trainers! They're knowledgeable, friendly, and informed about your local selling environment.

Here's how you redeem YOUR FREE SEMINAR invitation.

1. Go to www.Sandler.com and click on Find Training Location (top blue bar).
2. Select your location.
3. Review the list of all the Sandler trainers in your area.
4. Call your local Sandler trainer, mention *From the Board Room to the Living Room* and reserve your place at the next seminar!